Physical Characteristics of the Chihuahua

(from the American Kennel Club breed standard)

Body: Ribs rounded and well sprung.

Tail: Moderately long, carried sickle either up or out, or in a loop over the back, with tip just touching the back.

Hindquarters: Muscular, with hocks well apart, neither out nor in, well let down, firm and sturdy. The feet are as in front.

Coat: In the Smooth Coats, the coat should be of soft texture, close and glossy. Coat placed well over body with ruff on neck preferred, and more scanty on head and ears. Hair on tail preferred furry.

Pasterns: Fine.

Weight: A well balanced little dog not to exceed 6 pounds.

Color: Any color— Solid, marked or splashed.

Chihuahua

◇

by Barbara J. Andrews

Contents

KENNEL CLUB BOOKS® **CHIHUAHUA**
ISBN: 1-59378-239-X

Copyright © 2003, **2007** • Kennel Club Books® • A Division of BowTie, Inc.
40 Main Street, Freehold, NJ 07728 USA
Cover Design Patented: US 6,435,559 B2 • Printed in South Korea

Photographs by Isabelle Français and Carol Ann Johnson
with additional photos by:
Barbara J. Andrews, Norvia Behling, T. J. Calhoun, Carolina Biological Supply,
Doskocil, Graham & Margaret Foote, John Hartley, James Hayden-Yoav,
James R. Hayden, RBP, Bill Jonas, Dwight R. Kuhn, Dr. Dennis Kunkel,
Ken Lucas/Visuals Unlimited, Mikki Pet Products, Phototake, Jean Claude Revy,
Dr. Andrew Spielman, Alice van Kempen and C. James Webb.

Illustrations by Renée Low

DEDICATION

*This work is dedicated to Bill
Andrews and Dan Greenwald,
without whom this volume
would not have been possible.
They are Best Friends, as
generous and supportive as the
little dog in my sombrero. There
can be no greater compliment!*

—BARBARA J. ANDREWS

CHIHUAHUA

It is as difficult to imagine an evolutionary relationship between the Chihuahua and the St. Bernard as it is to accept that the Grizzly bear of North America is also of the same family.

Even stranger, the Chihuahua can be as diminutive as the smallest member of its family tree. The fennec averages only 3 lbs. Unable to agree on species classifi-cation because of features that do not conform to the fox, scientists finally assigned it a separate genus, *Fennecus zerda*. The fennec has extraordinarily large ears and big round "baby" eyes. Naturalists theorize that the incredibly oversized ears serve as shade during the rare times that the nocturnal fennec is exposed to sunlight. More importantly, heavy

The Longcoat Chihuahua has become twice as popular as the Smoothcoat. These three Longs represent three generations of well-bred Chihuahuas.

9

Chihuahua

PHOTO BY KEN LUCAS / VISUALS UNLIMITED.

dew produced by cold offshore currents would collect on the backs of the ears, which may explain how the tiny creature can survive indefinitely far from any known source of water.

While there may not be an evolutionary connection between the two tiny desert-dwellers, there are surprising similarities between the Chihuahua and the fennec fox. With his huge eyes and ears, the tiny Chihuahua is every bit as appealing as the endangered fennec fox, which sadly is now on Appendix Two of the CITES list. As the origin of the Chihuahua remains a much-debated mystery, it may be fun to hold in your mind these fascinating similarities.

Fennecus zerda has long, thin,

well-furred and somewhat flat feet that enable it to scoot about on top of the shifting sands. So did the early Chihuahua. The fennec is native to the desert zone from southern Morocco to Egypt and the Sudan. Many breed experts believe that this is exactly where the Chihuahua's ancestors originated. The little dogs are noted for not only recognizing but also needing other Chihuahuas. Totally unlike other foxes, the fennec chooses to live in groups of eight to ten.

The Chihuahua prefers a varied diet. Given the opportunity, he seeks precisely the same food as does the fennec: vegetation, (very!) small rodents, lizards and insects. Ask any Chihuahua owner about the breed's irresistible, irrepressible urge to chase and eat bugs! Like the Chihuahua, the little fox has weak dentition, a very rare condition in a wild species, yet unfortunately a common one in small dogs.

Who knows what may have occurred a thousand years ago? We do know that in the 1980s, the fennec was successfully crossed with a domestic dog breed. Need you ask which one? Such matings continue in California where, coincidentally, in the 1970s, the Asian leopard cat was mated to domestic cats. A medical researcher from the University of California discovered that the leopard cat is immune to leukemia but he was unable to handle or breed the small leopard for research purposes. Working with cat breeder Jean Mill, they achieved the allegedly impossible feat of combining the different number of chromosomes and overcoming other species incompatibilities. The spectacularly spotted result is the Bengal, a popular show cat and house kitty!

So come, let's have a look at some of the theories, legends and facts that contribute to the appeal of the world's smallest member of *Canis familiaris.*

Some breed historians believe that the ancestor of the Chihuahua was a hairless dog that came from Asia, across Russia, through the Bering Straits and into what is now Alaska. Hairless dogs existed in China, Africa and Turkey, and another theory has it that the Chinese Crested was "Americanized" as early as the seventh century BC when Chinese vessels reached Central and North American shores. Perhaps, but common sense makes one wonder if the Chinese had brought dogs with them, why would they give space and food to small, delicate, hairless pets rather than to the fat, hardy Chow Chows that could have fed the crews during a very long voyage? And what would they have had to sail in order to bring enough dogs to have influenced the genetic base in America? A doggy Noah's Ark?

Other researchers point to ancient hairless dogs that existed in Mexico and Central and South America. Evidence suggests that

The Chinese Crested has been linked to the Chihuahua as one of its possible "naked" ancestors. This toy breed is the most popular hairless dog in the world.

SMART LAP-WARMER

Since dogs have been inbred for centuries, their physical and mental characteristics are constantly being changed to suit man's desires for hunting, retrieving, scenting, guarding and warming their masters' laps. During the past 150 years, dogs have been judged according to physical characteristics as well as functional abilities. Few breeds can boast a genuine balance between physique, working ability and temperament.

they were always domesticated; well, at least since they became hairless! Folklore surrounding the Xoloitzcuintli has become confusingly interwoven with that of the Chihuahua, but the smallest size Xolo recognized by the Federacíon Canofila Mexicana and the Fédération Cynologique Internationale is twice the size of the largest Chihuahua! Only in America, where it is not recognized by the American Kennel Club, is a toy-sized Xolo described in a breed standard.

If we continue this circular logic, then why not suppose that the Peruvian and Mexican hairless dogs influenced the Chinese dogs and not the other way around? Small hairless dogs, some with a "top knot" of hair, are depicted in ancient Mayan figurines. Perhaps captains of Chinese vessels were

fascinated by the hairless dogs of South America, where they first made port, or, subsequently, the tiny ones discovered in Mexico. Why would they not have taken a few back to China and other parts of the world? One-way traffic makes little sense and, as you shall see, there is evidence to the contrary.

Additionally, any seasoned dog breeder would reject a connection between hairless dogs and the Chihuahua based on major differences in conformation. The rectangular head shape of all hairless dogs is absolutely unlike that of the Chihuahua. All hairless dogs have long, round, whippy tails whereas the Chihuahua has a flattened, stiff, furry tail. The long claw-like feet of the early Chihuahua are not seen in any other breed. As we noted earlier, the Chihuahua doesn't resemble the St. Bernard either, but then we aren't trying to convince anyone that they were ever the same breed at some point in time!

If we accept that there is simply no evidence to substantiate that the Chihuahua is descended from hairless dogs or from Chinese dogs brought to South and Central America in fifth-century sailing vessels, then we must look for some other explanation.

It seems to me that there are more plausible theories that place the breed's ancient roots in Egypt

or the Sudan and that it migrated across the Bering Straits or was carried through the Mediterranean countries and thence to Malta. Physical evidence connects the Maltese "pocket dog" to the Chihuahua, but it could be that its American ancestor was dropped off on the island by the ancient mariners. The singular but easily verified characteristic shared by the pocket dog and the Chihuahua is the presence of the soft spot in the skull known as the molera. The cranial gap closes in other canines just as it does in the human infant, but in most adult Chihuahuas, the gap can be easily detected. The significance here is that the Chihuahua is the only breed that has the molera!

As with all speculation, there are interesting discrepancies in the theory that focuses on China or Europe as the origin of the Chihuahua. Small dogs of North America were revered by the earliest humans as evidenced by Indian Knoll, a two-acre site in Kentucky. In a single dig, Dr. William Web found 21 small dogs interred in graves dated 3000 BC. Among the 900 human graves, certain dogs obviously had special status and meaning to the community.

The Kentucky dig provides irrefutable evidence that dogs were domesticated in North America long before they could possibly have arrived on Chinese vessels making port in Mexico. Mexico adjoins the United States from the Gulf Coast to the Pacific. A journey from Kentucky to the region of Chihuahua, Mexico is less than 1,500 miles, "a walk in the wood" compared to the migratory route from the Far East to Alaska.

Furthermore, as recorded in the authoritative publication *Walker's Mammals of the World*, Fifth Edition, Volume II, the oldest documented remains of domestic dogs, dating from 11,000 and 12,000 years ago, were found, respectively, in Idaho and in Iraq, which borders Turkey and Arabia!

No dog historian awaited the migratory Asians, so we know not whether the Chihuahua ancestor arrived with them or if, having first met the Eskimo, the migrants moved south to Idaho and were greeted by the American Indian and his little dog. I can accept that theory as easily as I speculate that what might have come across the land-bridge with them was an evolutionary offshoot of the fennec fox. The only certainty is that the North American Indian had domesticated the dog thousands of years before the Chinese sailed into Acapulco. So, as I said earlier, perhaps it is the other way around. Perhaps, when the earliest explorers arrived from China, they took back with them the darling little dogs of Mexico that had continued the southward migration.

In any case, it seems certain that the Toltec Techichi is the more recent ancestor of today's Chihuahua. Some believe that the Techichi was actually a rodent, and language barriers preclude proof. The Toltecs created a splendid civilization dominating much of Mexico. They were the builders of the great Pyramid of the Sun, only 30 miles from where Mexico City stands today. One of their cities was Chichen Itza. When my husband and I stood there amid the ruins, we were moved not only by how advanced they were but also by how in tune they were with the seasons, the sky and the universe, as was evidenced by remains of astrological tracking. The Toltecs worked in metal and clay, spun cotton and spread the cult of their gentle god Quetzalcoatl. Their empire reached its zenith around 900 AD but was destroyed by foreign and civil wars.

The Toltec dog is represented in stone carvings that are part of a monastery known as Huejotzingo. Building parts include materials transported from the Aztec pyramids of Cholula. The monastery, constructed by Franciscan monks circa 1530, is situated between Mexico City and Puebla.

The Toltec reign gave way to the Aztecs, who seem to have adopted the Techichi and the hairless ones and used them for religious sacrifice. The Aztec used rattles and two types of ceremonial drums, the *huehuetl* or *tlapanhuechuetl* (vertical drum) and the *teponaztli* (horizontal drum). One interesting museum piece is a Moche rattle, wherein the head of the rattle is a perfect likeness of a modern Chihuahua head. A human head completes the handle. The little dogs were ascribed great religious significance by the Aztecs and, thus,

they were a persuasive token of esteem given to the gods.

As social advances occurred and staying alive became easier, the people had more time to spend upon such matters as breeding dogs. Archeological evidence shows that selective keeping of dogs progressed from possible edible interest to one of spiritual significance and, finally, to the ultimate luxury of providing nothing more than companionship to early man.

This bonding is clearly demonstrated in a figurine dated over 3,000 years ago. It depicts a little dog kissing a human face. It is understandable that

The hairless dog known in Mexico as the Xoloitzcuintli occurs in three sizes; the Standard is shown here.

15

Chihuahuas were interred with their masters, and archeologists have found remains of the breed in human graves in Mexico and the United States. A Mayan example of the pet Chihuahua is found in a model of a woman walking with a child, holding his hand, while in her other arm she holds a tiny dog. It is dated about 750 AD and resides at Tulane University in New Orleans.

So whether existent dogs of North America were the ancestors of the Chihuahua, whether they were brought in on Chinese trading vessels, or whether they originated in the Egyptian desert, we know that dogs closely resembling today's Chihuahua thrived in what is now northern Mexico.

Mexico claims this authenticity by having furnished a name for the breed and, in fact, the Mexican Natural History Museum offers what many consider to be indisputable proof that the Chihuahua was native to northern Mexico. A skeleton measuring only 7 inches in length is clearly that of a Chihuahua-type dog, right down to the domed skull and several molera (openings) in the skull.

These two American champions were exported to Britain where the Smoothcoat, Marjax's Jamie Windwalker at Ballybroke, owned by the Footes, became the first American dog to become a British champion.

So we have come full circle, history having brought us back to Mexico and the southern United States. It is unfortunate that the many dialects of the American Indian afforded little in the way of meaningful descriptions of native dogs. An incredibly creative artist, the Indian used symbolism more than realism and relied on the spoken record, the Story Teller, to pass the past from one generation to the next.

One such story clearly relates to the Chihuahua. It was believed that the little dog not only could be a companion in the next world but also could fulfill an even more serious responsibility for his owner. It was thought that the sins of the master were transferred to the dog so that the human could gain safe passage to the other world. Getting there was no easy task, even for a sin-free soul.

Fr. Bernardino de Sahugun, a Franciscan friar during the time of the Spanish Conquest, greatly admired the Aztecs. He made extensive writings and consequently recorded one version of a common legend that may account for a couple of modern-day oddities.... First, the story.

Writing of the little dog's spiritual assistance he said, "The deceased were burnt, encircled by all their clothing and belongings, but he who had nothing among his wretched belongings

"X" MARKS THE SPOT

The Chihuahua is not the only pure-bred dog to hail from Mexico. The Xoloitzcuintli is a unique Mexican dog that has no hair (or hardly any at all).

This sighthound-like dog appears in three sizes, Standard, Miniature and Toy; this latter is known as the Mexican Hairless.

went bare, and underwent much pain and suffered much in order to pass the place of the obsidian-bladed wings. And also they caused him to carry a little dog, a yellow one, and they fixed about its neck a loose cotton cord. It was said that he (the dog) bore the dead one across the place of the nine rivers in the Land of the Dead."

A Story Teller speaks of "a yellow one that wore a strand of slackly spun cotton for a collar. Men say that he takes the dead across the ninefold river to Meitlantecutli. There the waters are wide, dogs are the ferrymen, and when he recognizes his master, he leaps into the water in order to take him across."

Color is significant to every culture, and for the Aztecs, yellow is the color of death. So it was that the little yellow dogs were sacrificed that they might precede their masters to the other side. There they waited to aid their loved one across the ninth river.

When one experiences the utter devotion of a Chihuahua, it is easy to understand how such a highly developed culture could believe that a dog such as that would gladly assume the sins of his beloved person. Furthermore, that same little dog would faithfully await the arrival of his master and then act as courier to get his loved one into Aztec heaven.

Perhaps that is why Montezuma II, last of the Aztec rulers, is said to have had hundreds of Chihuahuas in his incredibly modern palace. Records describe the molera, so there is little doubt that the tiny dogs were pure Chihuahua.

More recently, is that why General Santa Ana (the dictator of Mexico who sold northern Mexico to the US in 1848) also kept large numbers of golden fawn Chihuahuas? They went with him into battle, no doubt to guide his soul across the ninth river should he be slain. In fact, they were in his camp when he was finally defeated and captured in 1836.

The theory that places the Chihuahua's development in Europe, with the assumption that it arrived in the New World in the arms of Spanish explorers, totally ignores recorded history. The Spanish had a singular use for dogs during that time. They brought horses to the Americas, not dogs. When there was no local game, when there were no injured horses to be slaughtered, they raided Indian settlements for food that included indigenous camp dogs and, in some tribes, the small dogs kept for sacrifice—or as pets.

An early explorer of North America, Hernando de Soto, wrote that dogs were a major source of meat for the hundreds of troops he led during exploration of the southeastern US. Spanish conquistadors not only decimated the Indian population from the Florida peninsula to Mexico but also wiped out thousands of dogs.

Spanish scribes recorded that male dogs were fattened on corn, castrated and used for food by the Aztecs. No doubt they were used in religious ceremonies but, perusing the Spaniard's account, one has to wonder if, in fact, the

Indians were forced to breed them in great numbers in order to feed the conquistadors who enslaved them.

There is no reliable pictorial evidence of a Chihuahua-type dog in Europe before Columbus discovered America and subsequent explorations occurred. There is a painting by Botticelli dated 1481, which is displayed in the Sistine Chapel fresco. Having long, claw-like toes, the dog is said to be of Chihuahua type, but fanciers of the Bull Terrier claim it is an early ancestor of the White English Terrier. Discussion has also centered about the Pietro Longhi painting in Venice because it too depicts a Chihuahua-like family pet. Speculation is that the little female is a descendant of a Mexican dog brought back to Europe by a kind-hearted conquering hero!

In fact, it is probable that the tiny smooth-coated dog was mated to European spaniels, thus producing other delightful small breeds. These newer types, when mated back to the Chihuahua, along with a dash of tiny Pomeranian-like spitzen and other lap-sized dogs of the day, produced the long-haired Chihuahua and may be to blame for shortening the previously oversized ears.

In addition to searching for the city of gold, the Spaniards tried to convert the Indian

YOU SAY PODENGO, I SAY PODENGO

How does this terrier-type Portuguese dog figure into the origins of the Chihuahua? The

Podengo Portugueso comes in three sizes, the smallest of which appears very similar to the Chihuahua, though he can weigh as much as 12 pounds. The Pequeño variety is used to hunt rabbits and to exterminate rats. All three varieties exhibit both smooth and wirehaired coats.

population to Christianity. They employed many barbaric means to accomplish this goal, including subversion of the deeply held religious beliefs of the people they enslaved. They prohibited the use of dogs for sacrifice and feasting but it was several decades before these practices were successfully abolished. Records from the Augustin Mission some twenty years after the Conquest of 1539 describe the Aztec dog market at Acolhuan. It is said that dogs were sold strictly for food, usually eaten as part of special ceremonies such as weddings, funerals and other religious feasts.

In 1578, Francisco Hernandez described a dog that he said was the Techichi. He wrote that it was raised by the Indians as a food source, stating that they ate the small dogs just as the Spaniards ate rabbits. Maybe scribes in the 16th century didn't play around with the facts, only with the reasons behind those facts.

Having stood in the 17th-century church of San Esteban, high atop a 600-foot pinnacle called Acoma, or more commonly today, Sky City, I am inclined to think that the small quiet people so effectively enslaved by the Spaniards might have eaten or sold anything to survive! Not far west of Albuquerque, New Mexico, Acoma is the oldest inhabited settlement in the US, well established when the Spaniards first found it in 1540. The people there are poor and primitive. Water is still collected in the baked clay depressions scattered throughout the tiny community. The few people who emerge from the shadow of their adobe dwellings to be photographed or to sell their beautiful pottery seem quietly indulgent of and very removed from the

tourists. Very much remembering the reign of torture suffered under their white rulers, they were forced to shoulder massive timbers with which the church was built and carry them for a hundred miles across baked desert without allowing them to touch the earth. We saw no dogs, only the shadow of those that might have been....

Surely some were too small to be noticed by the cruel conquistadors or perhaps they were not considered worth the trouble to roast. The smallest and dearest would have been hidden in the high dwellings of the Pueblo people. Of this we can be certain: every Chihuahua owner is deeply grateful that the tiny desert-dwelling dogs escaped the voracious appetites of the Spaniards!

CURRENT HISTORY

The first record of the Chihuahua as a specific breed seems to have occurred about 1884 when enterprising Mexicans began selling them to tourists in the border markets. Tiny dogs were called Mexican, Texas and Arizona dogs, depending on whose soil one stood at the moment. Gradually, they became firmly associated with the Mexican State of Chihuahua just south of the border, and the little dog that knew no boundaries became known as the Chihuahua.

A dog show judge is said to have bought a dog in El Paso, Texas and, later, another from Tucson, Arizona. Mr. Watson authored a two-volume work on dogs but, even though the breed had been recognized in the US in 1903, he neglected to make mention of the Chihuahua in his book. So much for him!

The first Chihuahua to be officially registered was a dog called Midget, who entered the American Kennel Club Stud Book in 1904 along with three others. The UK was not far behind, with registration in 1907. Mexico entered the modern dog world a bit late but it granted registration privileges to the Chihuahua in 1934.

By 1915, 30 Chihuahuas were registered in the US and that number jumped to over 25,000 by the early 1970s! The breed is more popular in Europe and America than in Mexico, no doubt because anything "foreign" is always better than what's always been right under one's nose!

One of the first well-known sires was Caranza, possibly named for the President of Mexico. The red long-coated dog resided in Pennsylvania, where he met an untimely death in the jaws of a Great Dane, who, it is said, mistook him for a squirrel! Fortunately, this occurred after he had sired Meron and Perrito, both of which went on to become

What could be more delightful than a Chihuahua-filled bandana?

the foundation of two great American lines. The Perrito line died out in the late 1920s, but his influence was greatly prized in subsequent generations. Most breed authorities agree that Caranza, though registered, could not possibly have been pure-bred as there were no long-coated Chihuahuas in Mexico until about 1959. Indeed, it took 29 years after the Chihuahua Club of America was formed in 1923 before a separate Longcoat club came into existence.

The long and smooth coats were shown together until 1952, when they were separated into two varieties for the show ring. They are still interbred in the US, resulting in both coat varieties appearing in the same litter.

Well over 20,000 Chihuahuas are registered each year with the AKC. Only a fraction of those are

Chihuahua

Miss Lupe Velez, a famous actress of the 1930s, with her Chihuahua named King, being fed from his mistress's eye-dropper.

exhibited but they remain extremely, popular because they are such wonderful companions and because breeders strive to retain the breed's unique characteristics for the world to enjoy.

THE BREED IN ENGLAND

Representatives of the breed moved into England from the United States and directly from Mexico in the late 19th century. In 1897, a Chihuahua was formally exhibited at the Ladies Kennel Club Show. Registration privileges followed in 1907, which would appear to be a meteoric rise to fame except that it was 17 years before the next Chihuahua was registered!

Fewer than 100 were recorded by the beginning of World War II. The low breeding population was critically impacted by the bombing and devastation that followed. By 1949, there remained only eight registered Chihuahuas.

The famed Florence Clark with her Chihuahua champions that won prizes in the 1934 Westminster Kennel Club Show in New York, which attracted 2,462 entries. This was at the height of the Depression in America.

As families and homes were re-established, many turned back to dogs for solace and a logical choice was the Chihuahua. Easily fitting in cramped quarters during the rebuilding, he was inexpensive to feed and maintain, hardy, requiring few veterinary visits, and, above all, a grateful little soul to fill the empty arms and hearts of those who had suffered terrible losses. Numbers climbed rapidly and by 1953 there were 111 registered with The Kennel Club.

Due to a strike by electricians, the 1954 Crufts Dog Show had to be cancelled, so the first Challenge Certificates (awards needed to become a champion) actually were awarded by the Scottish Kennel Club at the Glasgow show. In a dead heat for

Thanks to modern advances in veterinary Cesarean techniques, Chihuahua births became less risky for the dam and breeder.

the title of first Champion of Record, the breed entered the record books as the two top Chihuahua contenders actually attained their titles at the same show on the same day! And even more dramatic, Mrs. Fearfield's Isabella and Mrs. Gray's Diaz did so at the last show of the year.

By 1965, the breed was split into Longcoat and Smoothcoat varieties with 159 Smooths and 87 Longs entered at Crufts that year. Total numbers recorded had exploded to over 3,000 due to advances in veterinary Cesarean techniques.

The next few decades saw Chihuahua population numbers and popularity continue to rise in spite of its being a breed averaging so few pups per litter. From the

UK, popularity spread to other European countries and, by the late 1970s, it was obvious that the little Mexican dog had found a welcome home in Europe!

A Chihuahua and a Bull Terrier can get along well together if they have been properly socialized.

CHIHUAHUA

Each breed is unique, which is why my husband and I have enjoyed six breeds in our more than forty years of active participation in the dog sport. As a young child, my heart was owned by an English Springer Spaniel named "Babe." She was a Christmas present, and though I would have been just as thrilled with a horse, my father chose wisely. The dog enabled us to share something wonderful at a time when an only child needed to know her father.

My teenage years with an English Setter ended when she was struck by a car. It seems like yesterday that I knelt in the busy street, wailing in despair. When my mother pulled her from my arms, I thought I would die. Forty years later, I held fast to a very special Akita, but even my grown-up arms were not strong enough to keep him in my world.

Why do we allow ourselves

Chihuahuas are social animals that prefer associating with veritable bands of dogs. Most owners of Chihuahuas have at least two of these Mexican darlings in their homes.

A REASON & A RUFF

Nothing is worse than a watchdog that barks at the neighbor's cat. When the Chihuahua barks, however, the reason is worth investigating!

to be so emotionally destroyed again and again? I suppose it's because we invite these dogs into our lives and because the brief time we have with them brings us much more than is taken away when the Creator calls in the loan. So if your next best friend is a little *perro* with a saucy expression and dancing feet, treasure each chuckle, each moment of comfort that he gives you, and know that he will be with you for a long time.

We are drawn to certain breeds because of size, personality or coat type. Much will depend on your age and lifestyle at the time. It is hoped that you are reading this book because you have decided to approach ownership thoughtfully and plan a long-term commitment. If your choice is the Chihuahua, it will be a long friendship as the breed commonly lives well past ten years.

No matter how much research you do, falling in love can still happen by chance. Owning a Chihuahua was the last thing I expected even though grooming big hairy dogs and running full-tilt around the show ring had me thinking about the practicality of a smaller breed. We continued to cast speculative glances at smaller dogs but none really excited me.

Then, while on the way to

MEN LOVE CHIHUAHUAS!

Famed band leader Xavier Cugat never went anywhere without the company of his tiny pack. Men who are confident in their own masculinity are quite willing to become acquainted with a "lap dog." Having done so, they are hooked!

ringside, I spied an excited group of people and detoured to see what was happening. Pushing my way between a very large lady and a pogo-stick (which turned out to be a little girl bouncing up and down in constrained enthusiasm), I saw what had drawn the crowd. I too wanted to reach down and scoop them all up but, like the child, I knew better. They were incredibly cute! Fluffy elfin creatures and sleek doe-like babies in a kaleidoscope of gorgeous colors!

Entranced, I realized that they weren't barking. In another ex-pen, there were several silent adults watching and wagging, and I wondered why I'd accepted the stereotype of "yappy ankle biters." Just as I was readjusting my perceptions, suddenly there erupted a ferocious barking as the adults squared off with an Irish Wolfhound, whose owner had pushed through to see the pups. The males were braced side to

TEX-MEX CLAN

By and large, this small breed is the most gregarious of all dogs—some even say clannish! More so than any other breed, Chihuahuas actually require company.

side, stiff-legged, ruffs ridged, tails up and vibrating as they dared the giant intruder to take just one more step! This was truly the dog world's equivalent of a Jonathan Swift battle of the Lilliputians and the Brobdingnagian. The girls bounced back and forth, barking encouragement while threatening to bite off the monster's toe. Everyone laughed as I continued to re-evaluate what I thought I knew about the littlest breed!

When the crowd had finally departed, I stayed to talk with the breeder and it became increasingly apparent that a fortuitous change of direction had afforded me a whole new perspective. She let me hold a puppy and I had found our "smaller" breed.

Living with the Chihuahua has caused many erroneous conceptions to fall away. For example, we often think of toy dogs as being weak or sickly. While they can't be allowed to romp with large dogs and dropping a ChiChi is likely to result in serious injury, the breed is far from delicate. They are the best watchdogs on our property, which is also guarded by Akitas and Miniature Bull Terriers. Whether inside or in the ChiChi house adjoining the bedroom, the only time that they bark is when something is amiss. When the Akitas bark at night, we roll over and go back to sleep. It is only a deer or some other night creature that they see frequently. If the Chihuahuas join in, we get up to check!

On one such occasion, the flashlight illuminated huge gold eyes in the rolling expanse just before a wooded copse. Standing on the bedroom balcony, my husband Bill fired a shot skyward. The eyes blinked and the Chihuahuas barked one last "so there!" and that was that.

On another moonless night, the ChiChis alerted us although the other dogs were quietly snoozing. Puzzled, Bill checked from inside the house and, seeing and hearing nothing, was about to return to bed when he heard a metallic clink and saw tail lights in the equipment yard. Sure enough, one of our plumbers was quietly picking up a jetter machine for an emergency call. When he started the truck to pull out, the big dogs roused and barked ferociously, but by then the Chihuahuas were quiet. They had done their job and when they knew that Bill was aware of the "problem," they returned to their sleep.

Chihuahuas are blessed with a strong immune system, overall hardiness and very few genetic defects. They are also less afflicted by the effects of bantamization than are other toy breeds. Perhaps because they have been tiny for so long? Who knows?

Small dogs have a higher metabolism and are therefore more affected by extreme heat or cold, yet the Chihuahua is remarkably unperturbed by either. For example, our dog family is comprised of three Akitas, six Mini-Bull Terriers and four Chihuahuas. This provides a unique opportunity to observe large Arctic-coated and small short-coated dogs in exactly the same environment, a situation that is often good for a laugh.

When the sun is blazing, the ChiChis are basking, the Mini-Bulls alternate between sun and shade and the Akitas are decidedly unhappy even though shaded by the roof. Invite them to play and the ChiChis fly around like little bullets, the Mini-Bulls go happily sponging after them and the Akitas refuse to move.

When it's snowing and blowing, the ChiChis are contentedly snuggled in bed, the Minis are shivering and the Akitas are smiling. No surprise! But again, invite them for a romp in the yard and the Chihuahuas and Akitas are thrilled to come out and play,

¡QUEREMOS EL SOL!

Chihuahuas are sun-worshippers and will bask in the sun for hours. They will find that little pool of warm sun even when kept indoors.

SOUND AN ALARM!

Chihuahuas make reliable and excellent alarm dogs. They will vociferously challenge strangers in their home territory.

while the Mini-Bulls are polite for only about ten minutes before they sneak back to bed.

The point is that despite their size and in direct contradiction to our tendency to spoil them, the Chihuahua is the most adaptable breed we have ever owned! Rain or shine, hot or cold, their thermostat works perfectly. This should come as no surprise, for the desert is fiercely hot during the day but temperatures can plummet to below freezing at night.

A note of caution: Common sense must prevail. Left to his own good judgment, the little dog won't go sledding in a

blizzard or beach-hopping in the mid-day sun. If we tempt them into foolhardy activities contrary to their instincts, then we should dry and warm the wet dog or cool down the overheated dog.

All our dogs are fed exactly alike, although proportionately. The Chihuahuas receive a bit more people food such as peas, green beans and fruit. They prefer a more varied diet and we indulge them because they are omnivorous gourmets, displaying a decided attraction to fresh foods over canned or dry. A properly reared Chihuahua will eat anything that is natural, wholesome and nutritious as opposed to some breeds that will select a scoop of ice cream over raw chicken or a cricket!

He rarely shivers from fear or cold but will tremble if nervous or excited. You will soon come to know what triggers the response. If he is uneasy in a strange situation, don't praise him. "It's OK, darling, mommy loves you" sounds like praise. It's best to laugh to reassure him there is nothing to be concerned about. If his safety is actually jeopardized, pick him up but try to maintain a casual attitude, not one of "Oh dear, let mommy protect the baby," which would only reinforce his fear.

And the Chihuahua should be fearless, i.e., terrier-like. Sometimes you wish he had a little better judgment, such as when he takes a high dive from the sofa before he's grown enough to handle the landing or when he flies in the face of a large aggressive dog. Lend him a little of your common sense. Don't put him on the couch and walk away when he's a puppy. Never let him go at a large dog. It could be fatal.

When held in your arms, he can be very aggressive toward other people. OK, so it is cute—after all, he's protecting you, the love of his life, but be careful that your "No" doesn't sound like "OK, how cute!" when you correct such unacceptable behavior.

The Chihuahua is an incredibly loyal friend. You are his world, not because he fears being out there all alone as do some toy dogs, but because regarding you as the center of his universe is a breed characteristic! Was it developed by centuries of human selection for the trait? I think not. There are other equally ancient breeds that will happily leave their human to chase a rabbit or explore the next horizon. The Chihuahua actually prefers your company to that of other dogs. Think about that. Most dogs will continue to play together when

DOGS, DOGS, GOOD FOR YOUR HEART!

People usually purchase dogs for companionship, but studies show that dogs can help to improve their owners' health and level of activity, as well as lower a human's risk of coronary

heart disease. Without even realizing it, when a person puts time into exercising, grooming and feeding a dog, he also puts more time into his own personal health care. Dog owners establish more routine schedules for their dogs to follow, which can have positive effects on their health. Dogs also teach us patience, offer unconditional love and provide the joy of having a furry friend to pet!

their owners call. Most children will continue to play when moms calls. Your Chihuahua will stop, ask if you really mean it and then fly into your arms! He would rather be snuggled next to you than chasing a butterfly. He requires touching,

29

Chihuahua

petting, conversation and your approval. Never too pushy, he will employ clever tricks to get your attention. If you are too busy to be amused or talked into a cuddle, he will just lie down close to you and wait.

ChiChis are very sociable with their own kind and two or more males can get along well, although you may have to forgive a bit of marking behavior when there is a female in season. Females will establish a pecking order and then show great affection for one another.

They love to sleep under a sheet or blanket and will even burrow under pillows in order to feel covered. Can this be a retained instinct from a

burrowing desert dweller? Although some other breeds like to be covered, none seems so determined as the Chihuahua.

Seeking sunlight is another highly developed compulsion in this breed. It's comical to watch your Chihuahua curl up in a tiny spot of warmth by the window and then observe his annoyance when he awakens to find that the spot has moved and left him in the shade!

Chihuahuas are ideal for single people, the elderly, the handicapped and shut-ins. They want nothing more than to be with their person and are especially perceptive of human moods. Moved to silent tears by a TV movie, I was brought back to the present by a gentle and reassuring kiss from the ChiChi that had been snoozing in my lap. If you are reading or napping, they will lie quietly, waiting, very aware of you. If you are moving from room to room, there is no need to look for your little friend. If you can't see him, it is because he is standing right at your heel, waiting to see which way you are going next.

According to an article published in *Our Dogs* in 1904, well-known singer Rosina Casselli stated that her Mexican Chihuahuas never got distemper. Other records, including those of Señora Dolores Gonzalez, bear out this amazing truth. This was so firmly known that even when the disease was common throughout Europe, Chihuahua owners rarely inoculated their dogs.

This does not suggest that your dog should be deprived of today's perfected vaccines; however, you might wish to discuss with your vet the possibility of a three-year vaccination program rather than yearly. It would be prudent to consider the long lifespan of the breed. A dog with a life expectancy of seven years will receive only half as many challenges to its immune system as compared to your little dog.

You can tell a Chihuahua lover by the smile on her face!

More breeders and vets are rethinking the necessity of yearly vaccinations.

In all, the Chihuahua is an amazingly hardy and disease-free pure-bred. Certain small-dog problems have been reported, including cleft palates and hypoglycemia, the former of which affects newborn puppies. Other problems include hemophilia A, secondary glaucoma, certain heart-valve problems, lung problems and hydrocephalus. Discuss these health issues with the breeder before making a final decision about buying a pup from his line.

You should discuss health issues with the breeder of your Chihuahua. Many problems can be avoided if healthy parents have produced your puppy.

Chihuahua

Whether adorned in long or smooth coats, Chihuahuas offer many things to many people. Consider the rainbow of Chihuahua colors from which you can choose. Any one of these delightful dogs could brighten up your rainiest days.

BREED STANDARD FOR THE

CHIHUAHUA

Think of the breed standard as a recipe for perfection. Instead of ingredients arranged in the order to be included, the features that make the Chihuahua a feast for the eyes and soul are listed in the order of importance.

First, a general description. Is it large, fearsome, friendly, etc.? After all, we wouldn't want a Mastiff to be as energetic as the Chihuahua, nor would our little friend be correct if he were as placid as the Basset Hound. Temperament is described because, unlike behavior that is influenced by environment, schooling or the like, each breed has an inherited personality.

We most often look at our dog's face as we communicate with him, just as he looks up at us. Therefore the standard explains what makes a Chihuahua's head unique. Certainly, the eye shape, placement and overall expression should say "Chihuahua." OK, now you know how to read the recipe, so let us put it all together.

The American and British standards are quite similar. The Mexican/FCI standard is more detailed. For example, not excusing problems commonly associated with dwarfing, it specifies that a deformity, deficiency or lack of harmony is to be faulted. It also states (correctly) that the breed is a companion and a guardian or alarm dog.

There is lively discussion regarding the differences between American and English Chihuahuas. Such comparisons are ongoing in all breeds—bigger here, higher stationed there, etc. The possibility that the stock of one country is superior to that of another isn't really an issue among most Chihuahua owners. It is only when one becomes involved in the breeding, showing and judging processes that minute differences (no pun intended) become gigantic debates.

British breeder, Mr. Graham Foote, gave a most interesting observation in one of the Chihuahua Club of America's handbooks. He wrote, "I recall admiring Tanya and Darwin Delaney for keeping their cool at the Windsor Show a few years ago when they were visiting the UK and a rather objectionable European lady was forcibly telling them that all American

The standard calls for a dog that is small, dainty and compact. The long coat should have a soft texture and can appear flat or slightly wavy.

Chihuahuas have legs that are too long; but I believe she actually admitted that she had never even visited the States."

Mr. Foote also pointed out that in America some dogs finish from the Puppy Class and, of course, they are a bit gangly and the briskets have not dropped. This tends to make them look somewhat longer in leg. Graham also explained that in America photographs are generally taken on the table whereas "in the UK most photographs are taken on the ground with the camera angle looking down on the dog which makes them look shorter in the leg and possibly longer in the back."

Sitting ringside at specialty shows in both countries, I saw no major differences in conformation or depth of quality. While on a recent trip to the UK, I was accompanied by a multi-group American judge. As we sat ringside at a large specialty, I asked her what, if any, differences she noted. She said that the dogs in America might be a "trifle sounder behind" whereas dogs in the UK were gloriously coated and wondered if the damp climate accounted for that. When I explained that the coat types are not interbred in England, she laughingly decided that any differences were more likely to be genetic than climatic.

In the following discussion of the breed standard and its

variations, points of the standard are indicated in bold, and the author comments on each point.

Under **General Appearance** Britain's Kennel Club standard is brief: "Small, dainty, compact." The American standard, revised in 1990, is a bit more eloquent, requiring a "graceful, alert, swift-moving little dog with saucy expression, compact, and with terrier-like qualities of temperament." To a knowledgeable dog person, reference to "terrier-like" is significant, but for those not familiar with terriers, it means tremendous heart, courage, tenacity and high intelligence.

Characteristics: "Everyone knows that" is too often the rationale for not placing more emphasis on the character traits that really define a breed. One of the most compelling breed characteristics is the god-like worship shown to his special person. Most toy breeds bond closely to people but not usually to the extent that a Chihuahua prefers human companionship over that of its own species.

Dan Greenwald, a good friend who has been more than successful in small breeds, says of this one, "The essence of the Chihuahua is not easily defined due to their many faces. It can not be fully realized until the actual hands-on, lived-with experience. To be fair, the judgment—the essence is in living with a Chihuahua."

"Generally speaking, a Chihuahua makes a marvelous companion—and for a good number of years, God willing. And by companion, I mean constant. They become incredibly attached to their family and within the family, an odd occurrence almost always takes place, and that is their selection of one special person.... their 'soul-mate'."

The standard describes an alert, swift-moving little dog, but then all tiny dogs must be swift-footed to avoid being stepped on! Seriously though, the Chihuahua moves with "brisk, forceful action," never does he just stroll about as might a Pekingese. A Chihuahua struts his stuff because he is a busy dog with exciting things to do and, while on the road to wherever it is, he believes no doubt that he owns every inch of the way!

Temperament is described as "gay, spirited and intelligent."

Indeed, the Chihuahua is perpetually happy. If he seems sad, he is either separated from his person or he is sick.

A Smooth male that placed in the group at a major UK dog show was a great example of proper temperament. Dorentys Nokumded Norman caught my eye as soon as he walked into the ring. He appeared ever so tiny but he had by far the biggest attitude as he pranced and strutted like a little stallion. Not at all intimidated by "the big ring," as it's known, he struck one pose after another and, when called upon to gait around the ring, he stepped out on that green carpet as though to say "Here, is everybody watching?" and then away he went to tumultuous applause, displaying excellent temperament, attitude and, yes, movement!

I can recall no breed described as less than intelligent; however, the standard fails to define the Mensa-like reasoning capability of the Chihuahua. As a former professional trainer, I am not just a doting owner who claims to have "the smartest dog in the world." For example, call any dog and (if he is so inclined) he will come to you in the shortest, most direct route. But suppose he cannot? Suppose there is a fence between you and the gate is some distance away in the other direction. Although I have always said that dogs can and do reason, they do not have great imaginative skills nor the ability to sort out complex problems, particularly if the solution requires an action contrary to instinct or previously learned behavior.

To train a Chihuahua to "go out" in obedience work is a challenge. He doesn't want to go away from you and he doesn't understand why you want him to do so. It takes patience and several days' work before an already well-schooled obedience champion finally understands that in order to be obedient, he is to run away from you! Now imagine, if you can, a dog that can immediately comprehend that incomprehensible fact!

The first time one of our Chihuahuas strayed into the two-acre exercise paddock, we learned just how big a brain that small dog has! My husband called and Howdy immediately ran to the fence closest to the garden but discovered he could go neither through nor over it. Without a moment's hesitation, he wheeled about, ran the other way, past the big-dog kennels, through the open gate, and came to a skidding stop in front of two speechless people!

As we stood there absorbing the significance of what we had witnessed, Bill pointed at Ginny and Icey standing on the other side of the fence with puzzled expressions, no doubt wondering why Howdy had left in such a hurry. Bill called. They glanced at each other as though to say, "We can't jump that fence, can we?" then simultaneously, they whirled and repeated Howdy's incredible feat.

So it hadn't been just a coincidence! That was the defining moment when Bill stopped teasing me about my "lap dogs." As they danced around our feet, Howdy lifted his leg on a potted plant as much as to say "Nothing to it." Would any other dog in my kennel have figured it out so quickly? No. Would any other dog have figured it out at all? I doubt it—not without having accidentally found his way back through the gate at least once previously.

A Chihuahua owner who allows his dog to develop to his full potential rather than keeping him in a pen will have equally amazing stories to tell. And why not? Imagine long ago being the smallest dog living in close companionship with a creature not necessarily known for grace or good temper. Imagine the extreme climatic conditions, scarcity of food and water and being eaten by the creatures to whom you were inexplicably drawn. The little dog of the desert has not only survived, he has prospered.

The standard specifies that the breed should be neither "snappy nor withdrawn." No one would think of a Chihuahua as being withdrawn, but the standard has a bit of a breakdown in the public relations department. The Chihuahua is not to be trifled with when held in the arms of his owner. Oddly, he can even be defensive when held in the arms of a complete stranger! Chihuahua lovers chuckle and forgive these idiosyncrasies but you should never encourage this sort of behavior, particularly if you plan to exhibit the dog.

Head: It has been said that domesticated canines were genetically halted in evolutionary development. The theory is that the species was unconsciously selected for puppy-like traits that endeared them to their caveman masters. I'm not an anthropologist, but I have given that idea some thought. Maybe the cavewoman was less likely to club to death a puppy-like creature but, on the other hand, would her husband have welcomed it as a productive member of his family group? I think not. While beginning to appreciate the dog's superior sensory abilities and its endurance and stamina in the hunt, I suspect he would only have tossed a meat scrap to a dog capable of hunting large game. That animal would hardly be puppy-like in its nature. It would be fierce and predatory. So when was it that early man decided that baby appeal was more important than the ability to hunt, guard and herd?

Oh, well, we will leave that to scientists to sort out, but

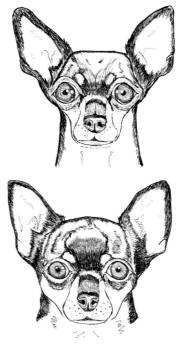

Undesirable head; skull flat and eyes protruding.

Correct head; smooth and "apple-domed."

somehow the notion that the wolf evolved into the tiny doe-eyed creature in your lap is a bit hard to accept—is it not? Perhaps those endearing physical features were present long before the wolf influence? Perhaps, as has been postulated by some anthropologists, the domestic dog carries the genes of the wolf, the hyena and the fox. One thing is certain—even the theory of human evolution is only that: a theory.

Indeed, the Chihuahua head is oversized, just like that of other mammalian infants. The rounded, baby-like shape of the skull is said to have occurred because of selective dwarfing of the breed.

37

Chihuahua

The Chihuahua is recognized by the "apple-domed" head that is different from the skulls of other dog breeds.

The very large, luminous eyes are preserved through selective breeding, but might we not once again take a speculative look at the fennec and other desert dwellers? They also have huge luminous, round "baby-like" eyes. Perhaps man had nothing to do with the Chihuahua's "arrested development" characteristics!

Head and expression define every pure-bred. We recognize a Bloodhound by his sad expression. A Bulldog is immediately identifiable as a "sourmug." The Chihuahua will be recognized by the apple-shaped head that is totally contrary to the natural rectangular shape of the canine skull. The large head presents a bit of a problem in whelping, but Nature's wise design allows the skull bones to flex as the whelp passes through the birth canal. In most mammals, including humans, the bones harden and knit together soon after birth. In the Chihuahua, there remains a small gap or molera in the top of the skull where the bones fail to join. The presence of the molera does not harm the dog. It is, however, unique to the Chihuahua dog, and it is significantly baby-like.

The same can be said for the **eyes**, which are the most prominent facial feature in the human infant. The nose is disproportionately tiny, enabling the infant to breathe while nursing

and also giving it a darling expression. The eyes and tiny little muzzle of the adult Chihuahua are just too childlike to resist!

The huge eyes do tear a bit more than a smaller eye. Tearing can be caused by a physical problem such as ingrown eyelashes but, in this case, tearing is a remarkable mechanism for flushing dust from the oversized surface of the eye. Whether the Chihuahua's roots lie in China, Egypt or the American Southwest, we know that his natural environment was the desert. Blowing sand and dry air demand more flushing than would the evolutionary environment of the Bull Terrier or Collie dog.

The eye color should be dark. Any indication of cloudy or blue tint may indicate an injury to the eye. In a very light-colored dog, one may observe the ruby eye, which in darkness will glow red! It is perfectly natural and considered yet one more unusual characteristic of an unusual breed.

The loss of those huge **ears**, which markedly set the breed apart from all but the fennec fox, is a great loss. "Large" is not defined. Large compared to the Pomeranian or large as compared to the German Shepherd? Large as compared to all other domestic dogs? Who are we to say? Were the composers of the standards in America and the UK more knowledgeable than those ancient civilizations that nurtured the huge-eared, long-footed tiny dog for thousands of years?

To the public (and that is who we should be concerned about), there are certain characteristics that define the Chihuahua as such. While breeders bemoaned the television commercials for the Mexican fast-food chain Taco Bell™, the public adores them! The little talking dog may not have the most perfect headpiece, but one thing that he has is the large, flaring ears that immediately distinguish him as a Chihuahua!

I have discussed this phenomenon with breeders on both sides of the Atlantic and I think most would agree with Dan Greenwald. He once said, laughing, "If I had to choose between a Chihuahua with perfect front, perfect rear and perfect size but with small ears and eyes, I would grab the Taco Bell™ dog!"

The **mouth** can be troublesome for breeders in that we strive to produce the correct number of teeth, properly aligned in a scissors bite. In other words, the top front teeth just barely overlap the front of the bottom teeth and the canine teeth or bottom fangs fit neatly into a slight indentation just in front of the top canines. Chihuahuas may have one or more missing teeth and, equally troublesome, they can lose premolars at a very young age, another of those odd characteristics shared with the fennec.

Undesirable ears; set too low and back.

Correct ears.

Whether dentition weakness is the result of overcrowding in a too-short muzzle is debatable. Looked at according to diet, tiny little dogs that never had to rip dinner from the carcass of a deer would not require a full mouth as would wolf-related breeds. This is not to forgive a faulty mouth but to simply point out that a little carnivore that existed on vegetation, birds and eggs, lizards and insects did not require the teeth of a Bull Terrier.

Use common sense as regards diet. Soft, easy-to-chew food for the older dog may be required but, if you are uncertain, try tossing your Chihuahua a raw chicken wing and see how well he handles it!

The **neck** should be arched and of medium length. To breeders, this means that in guarding against the short, thick "stuffy" neck, we must not breed for long swan-like necks. The neck is an extension of the spinal column and the breed should be slightly longer than tall but, remember, a long neck can't properly support a head as large in proportion to the body as the Chihuahua should have.

When viewed in profile, the **body** should show marked forechest. This does not mean a protruding sternum that can indicate serious abnormalities, but just a nice well-developed forechest. The front legs are set well under the dog so you can't

The Chihuahua should never appear overdone or cloddy. When viewed in profile, the forechest should be noticeable, without a protruding sternum.

see his chest from the side, meaning that the shoulders are too straight and too far forward. Good shoulders are important so that he can jump, bounce, change directions instantly (to catch that bug!) and, in all ways, be a superb little athlete.

The ribs should be well sprung but not so much as to make him appear overdone or cloddy. He needs plenty of room for his big heart and well-developed lungs. The rib cage should also be long enough to protect the internal organs. The underline should not rise before the seventh or eighth rib, at which point the profile should begin to show a slight tuck-up. Shallow, sausage-shaped bodies are extremely undesirable.

The **hindquarters** should be muscular with strong, well-defined tendons. The back leg has grooves in which the tendon fits and acts as a pulley to flex and extend the leg. If the grooves are too shallow or the tendon too thin, it can slip out of the groove, causing lameness. The joint and pulley design is as susceptible to injury as is the fine-tuned muscular knee of a football player. Therefore, never pull on the back legs and try to discourage jumping about in an upright position, particularly in the young dog. Chihuahuas do this so they can better communicate with you and be closer to the face they want to

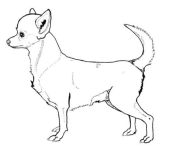

Undesirable body. Too square; stifle over-angulated.

Smoothcoat showing correct body type.

Longcoat showing correct body type.

kiss. Far better that you pick up your little friend than let him continue to dance on his hind legs.

All of this comes together in a body that is slightly longer than tall, which should have a level, flat, strong back. The frequency with which we see dogs with camel backs seems to have increased in the past few years and is something to which breeders should pay attention. The wheel-shaped back is associated with other structural faults of the neck, forequarters and hindquarters and also rather pushes the tail-set downwards so as to prevent its being set high and happy. Back length is important because a back too long will either sag or arch in compensation for stability's sake. Neither is a pretty sight. He should have balance that is both pleasing to the eye and functional. This cannot be achieved if the legs are bowed or crooked or if the neck and back are out of proportion. While it is his head and expression that we most often look at, we also see him trotting about the home and playing in the yard. He should be able to do so without thought or effort, which means that breeders must do their part to see that he is properly constructed.

The Chihuahua should be a superb athlete. When you step into the yard, he should be off like a shot, exploring and marking his territory. He is quite capable of keeping up with you on the longest walks. If his conformation is too faulty, he'll be at a disadvantage. That is another reason that we have a written description of the ideal structure for each breed.

The **feet** should be small and dainty with the toes not too tightly together. Whether soft sand

or adobe cliff dwelling, he needs plenty of foot on the ground to provide good traction. The really long toes are no longer seen, even though they would certainly be a distinguishing characteristic, particularly in the show ring where, in most breeds, a tight rounded foot is considered essential.

It has been my experience that breeders refer to specific breed features with great pride. The long, bony, claw-like toes are clearly distinguishable in old photographs. What utilitarian purpose could they have served? We know that the dog was better adapted to digging, as many other burrowing animals have elongated digging toes. So who decided that a more ordinary foot would better serve the Chihuahua? Why was it felt that long finger-like toes were detrimental to a breed that had survived for hundreds of years with that particular foot? Perhaps because it was so "different" than the more common "cat foot"? (That, too, has always puzzled me: if a tight round foot is correct for a dog, then why call it a *cat* foot?) In any case, what must have been a functional foot for a thousand years was replaced by modern judging preferences! The rather splayed, elongated foot of the wolf and coyote could no doubt also be improved upon if they were to become show dogs! Finally, in sad commentary on the long toes, Chihuahua breeders must work at maintaining the dainty short toes. All domestic dogs are affected by what is commonly referred to as "the drag of the breed." Unless breeders consciously and consistently select for manmade traits, all pure-bred dogs revert to their ancient characteristics. Flattened faces become longer. Long hound ears become shorter and upright. The Chihuahua foot becomes longer, thinner and flatter in succeeding generations. What does all this mean? Not much to the average owner. What may or may not have been functional a thousand years ago has little bearing on the genetically created dogs of today.

Unlike breeds that demand a small round foot, the nails of the Chihuahua need not be kept as short, but this does not mean that one can neglect a regular pedicure, excusing lack of care with "Oh, Chihuahua nails are supposed to be long." If he were running in his natural environ-ment, he would wear the nails back, but dancing on the carpet does nothing to wear down the nails; thus, you must take care of his feet. Excessively long nails will damage the toes, causing premature onset of orthopedic problems. Regular clipping with a little tool designed for the purpose or filing with a coarse board will accomplish the task. Begin nail care as a puppy and, when holding him, massage the paws so that he never becomes foot-sensitive.

The **tail** is a continuation of the spine, so it should be set high, carried up and over the back, never tucked under or curled below the topline. A peculiarity of the breed is the shape of his well-furred tail. The vertebrae are slightly flattened so that the tail has a fan-like appearance when viewed in profile. The bone, though not completely round, should be very strong and must not be twisted or kinked, which would be an indication of a weakness in the spinal column.

Undesirable Longcoat tail, tucked under body.

Correct tail for Longcoat, set high, carried over back.

Correct tail for Smoothcoat, set high, carried over back.

Undesirable tail carriage for Smoothcoat, curled below topline.

Tail carriage is a combination of two factors: skeletal structure and attitude. A terrier-like, feisty, confident, saucy, little athlete will carry his tail as proudly as the career soldier salutes the flag.

Any **color** or mixture of colors is accepted without preference.

This tricolored youngster shows off his long coat.

The strong terrier influence can still be seen in personality as well as in Chihuahuas with black and tan terrier markings, common in many terrier breeds. Also evident in some is the Papillon influence, freckles and a bit longer muzzle. The Pomeranian background is evidenced by the multitude of colors, smaller eyes and woolly coat.

The six-pound **size** limit is universally workable. Dogs can safely be smaller and have been bred from with success if they are masculine and well boned. Some very diminutive bitches have contributed as producers, some even being free-whelping, but most breeders prefer a brood matron to be on the upper weight limit. Conversely there have been more than a few that tipped the scales over when in hard condition but they have proved themselves in breeding programs on both sides of the Atlantic.

Note that the standard essentially says that no dog is perfect. They all have faults and, in the show ring, faults are weighed against virtues. In our hearts, we never see faults, and even our eyes are blind to any shortcomings. If you read this and look at your dog a bit differently, I hope it is only to appreciate his unique characteristics and his college degree in people-pleasing! He's the best at what he does, so if the ears are a bit short or he's on the largish side, it matters not—so long as he is a good little Chihuahua in his heart and actions.

What you have learned is that the Chihuahua is small in only one regard. He has the courage of a Great Dane, the proportionate strength of a Mastiff and the agility and athleticism of a Doberman Pinscher. His body fits in the palm of your hand but it contains a heart as big and strong as a Greyhound, and his capacity for absolute devotion and complete obedience to his special person is exceeded by no other animal in the universe!

What a *huge* gift to mankind he is!

CHIHUAHUA

Chihuahuas are not for everyone! That same statement applies to most breeds of dog as well as to dogs in general, but breeders feel especially strong about not selling Chihuahua puppies to just any interested buyer. Mr. Graham Foote says, "As a breeder I think that my Chihuahuas are not suitable pets for all homes. Initial inquiries generally come in by phone and I want to know as much as possible about the prospective owner before I let them come to see the puppies. I want to know if they have had a Chihuahua before, what happened to it, have they had other dogs before (or presently), do they have children, etc. I will not normally let my pups go to homes with girls under the age of eight years or boys under the age of twelve. Some breeders will not sell their dogs to elderly people but my experience has been that dogs and elderly people can be great companions for each other and I have never refused someone because of age. I do, however, always discuss the situation with prospective owners and tactfully say that

Chihuahuas can live a very long time, and while I hope they outlive their new pet, they must consider written arrangements for the care of the dog should they no longer be able to care for it."

"When I sell a Chihuahua, I always advise the new owners that the dog should not be excessively mollycoddled and to treat them as they would a larger dog. Our Chihuahuas run out in the snow, frost, rain and as long as they are running about there is no problem. Being so small, Chihuahuas can lose body heat quite rapidly and must not be left sitting out in the cold."

WHERE TO BEGIN?
If you are convinced that the Chihuahua is the ideal dog for you, it's time to learn about where to find a puppy and what to look for. Locating a litter of Chihuahuas should not present a problem for the new owner, as the breed is one of the more popular toy breeds in the world. You should inquire about breeders in your area who enjoy a good reputation in the breed. You are looking for an

45

ARE YOU PREPARED?

Unfortunately, when a puppy is bought by someone who does not take into consideration the time and attention that dog ownership requires, it is the puppy who suffers when he is either abandoned or placed in a shelter by a frustrated owner. So all of the "homework" you do in prepara-

tion for your pup's arrival will benefit you both. The more informed you are, the more you will know what to expect and the better equipped you will be to handle the ups and downs of raising a puppy. Hopefully, everyone in the household is willing to do his part in raising and caring for the pup. The anticipation of owning a dog often brings a lot of promises from excited family members: "I will walk him every day," "I will feed him," "I will house-train him," etc., but these things take time and effort, and promises can easily be forgotten once the novelty of the new pet has worn off.

established breeder with outstanding dog ethics and a strong commitment to the breed. New owners should have as many questions as they have doubts. An established breeder is indeed the one to answer your four million questions and make you comfortable with your choice of the Chihuahua. An established breeder will sell you a puppy at a fair price if, and only if, the breeder determines that you are a suitable, worthy owner of his/her dogs. An established breeder can be relied upon for advice, no matter what time of day or night. A reputable breeder will accept a puppy back, without questions, should you decide that this is not the right dog for you.

When choosing a breeder, reputation is much more important than convenience of location. Do not be overly impressed by breeders who run brag advertisements in the dog magazines about their stupendous champions. The real quality breeders are quiet and unassuming. You hear about them at the dog shows, by word of mouth.

It's recommended that you acquire a Chihuahua that is around ten to twelve weeks of age. Socialization is a breeder concern of considerable importance. Puppies that remain with their breeder for a few months may exhibit a lack of social graces and may not bond with a new owner as readily as the younger puppy.

Choosing a breeder is an important first step in dog ownership. Fortunately, the majority of Chihuahua breeders is devoted to the breed and its well-being. New owners should have little problem finding a reputable breeder who doesn't live in another state or on the other side of the country. The American Kennel Club is able to refer you to breeders of quality Chihuahuas, as can any local all-breed club or Chihuahua club. Potential owners are encouraged to attend dog shows to see the Chihuahuas strutting around the ring, to meet the owners and handlers firsthand and to get an idea of what Chihuahuas look like outside a photographer's lens. Provided you approach the handlers when they are not terribly busy with the dogs, most are more than willing to answer questions, recommend breeders and give advice.

Once you have contacted and met a breeder or two and made your choice about which breeder is best suited to your needs, it's time to visit the litter. Keep in mind that most top breeders have waiting lists, and given the small size of Chihuahua litters (one to four pups), these can be most disheartening. Sometimes new owners have to wait as long as

TEMPERAMENT COUNTS

Your selection of a good puppy can be determined by your needs. A show potential or a good pet? It is your choice. Every puppy, however, should be of good temperament. Although

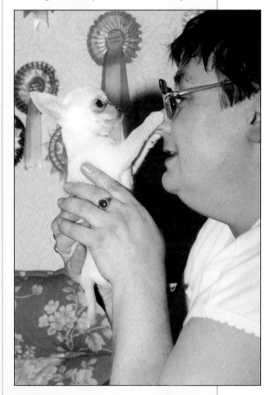

show-quality puppies are bred and raised with emphasis on physical conformation, responsible breeders strive for equally good temperament. Do not buy from a breeder who concentrates solely on physical beauty at the expense of personality.

INHERIT THE MIND

In order to know whether or not a puppy will fit into your lifestyle, you need to assess his personality. A good way to do this is to interact with his parents. Your pup inherits

not only his appearance but also his personality and temperament from his sire and dam. If the parents are fearful or overly aggressive, these same traits may show up in your puppy.

two to three years for a puppy. If you are very anxious (and truly prepared), you may have to resort to your second- or third-choice breeder. Use common sense. If the breeder doesn't have a waiting list, or any customers, there is probably a good reason. It's no different than visiting a restaurant with no clientele. The better restaurants always have a waiting list—and it's usually worth the wait. Besides, isn't a puppy more important than a great meal?

Since you are likely to be choosing a Chihuahua as a pet dog and not a show dog, you simply should select a pup that is friendly and attractive. The gender of your puppy is largely a matter of personal taste, as is coloration. As the many photographs in this book evidence, the breed comes in a multitude of lovely colors. The coat length of your Chihuahua is a more important consideration as the Longhair will require more grooming than the Smooth, though neither is very time-consuming.

Breeders commonly allow visitors to see the litter by around the fifth or sixth week, and puppies leave for their new homes between the tenth and twelfth week. Given the tiny size of the breed, and the dainty limbs and molera on the skull, breeders simply cannot afford to

PUPPY APPEARANCE

Your puppy should have a well-fed appearance but not a distended abdomen, which may indicate worms or incorrect feeding, or both. The body should be firm, with a solid feel. The skin of the abdomen should be pale pink and clean, without signs of scratching or rash. Check the hind legs to make certain that dewclaws were removed, if any were present at birth.

risk allowing new owners to adopt their new charges too early.

COMMITMENT OF OWNERSHIP

After considering all of these factors, you have most likely already made some very important decisions about selecting your puppy. You have chosen a Chihuahua, which means that you have decided which characteristics you want in a dog and what type of dog will best fit into your family and lifestyle. If you have selected a breeder, you have gone a step further—you have done your research and found a responsible, conscientious person who breeds quality Chihuahuas and who should be a reliable source of help as you and your puppy adjust to life together.

Visiting a litter will assist you in learning to recognize what a healthy pup should look like and

how pups interact and behave. A well-socialized Chihuahua will be anxious to meet new humans and will welcome an extended friendly hand and a warm lap.

Researching your breed, selecting a responsible breeder and observing a litter are all important steps on the way to dog ownership. It may seem like a lot of effort...and you have not even brought the pup home yet! Remember, though, you cannot be too careful when it comes to deciding on the type of dog you want and finding out about your prospective pup's background. Buying a puppy is not—or should not be—just another whimsical purchase. This is one instance in which you actually do get to

These Chihuahua babies are too young to receive visitors. Breeders commonly allow visitors around the fifth or sixth week.

PUPPY'S PAPERS

Too often new owners are confused between two important documents, the pedigree and the registration certificate. Your puppy's pedigree, essentially a family tree, is a written record of a dog's genealogy of three generations or more. The pedigree will show you the names as well as performance titles of all dogs in your pup's background (Ch., CD, CGC, etc.). Your breeder must provide you with a registration application, with his part properly filled out. You must complete the application and send it to the American Kennel Club (AKC) with the proper fee. The seller must provide you with complete records to identify the puppy. The AKC requires that the seller provide the buyer with the following: breed; sex, color and markings; date of birth; litter number (when available); names and registration numbers of the parents; breeder's name; and date sold or delivered.

buying a puppy is a pleasurable and exciting endeavor, it is not something to be taken lightly. Relax…the fun will start when the pup comes home!

Always keep in mind that a puppy is nothing more than a baby in a furry disguise…a baby who is virtually helpless in a human world and who trusts his owner for fulfillment of his basic needs for survival. In addition to food, water and shelter, your pup needs care, protection, guidance and love. If you are not prepared to commit to this, then you are not prepared to own a dog, particularly a Chihuahua who lives for the love of his master or mistress.

PREPARING PUPPY'S PLACE IN YOUR HOME

Researching your breed and finding a breeder are only two aspects of the "homework" you will have to do before taking your Chihuahua puppy home. You will also have to prepare your home and family for the new addition. Much as you would prepare a nursery for a newborn baby, you will need to designate a place in your home that will be the puppy's own. How you prepare your home will depend on how much freedom the dog will be allowed. Whatever you decide, you must ensure that he has a place that he can "call his own."

choose your own family! You may be thinking that buying a puppy should be fun—it should not be so serious and so much work. Keep in mind that your puppy is not a cuddly stuffed toy or decorative ornament, but a creature that will become a real member of your family. You will come to realize that, while

When you bring your new puppy into your home, you are bringing him into what will become his home as well. Obviously, you did not buy a puppy so that he could take control of your house, but in order for a puppy to grow into a stable, well-adjusted dog, he has to feel comfortable in his surroundings. Remember, he is leaving the warmth and security of his mother and littermates, as well as the familiarity of the only place he has ever known, so it is important to make his transition as easy as possible. By preparing a place in your home for the puppy, you are making him feel as welcome as possible in a strange new place. It should not take him long to get used to it, but the sudden shock of being transplanted is somewhat traumatic for a young pup. Imagine how a small child would feel in the same situation—that is how your puppy must be feeling. It is up to you to reassure him and to let him know, "Little *amigo*, you are going to like it here!"

WHAT YOU SHOULD BUY

CRATE

To someone unfamiliar with the use of crates in dog training, it may seem like punishment to shut a dog in a crate, but this is not the case at all. Most experi-

QUALITY FOOD

The cost of food must be mentioned. All dogs need a good-quality food with an adequate supply of protein to develop their bones and muscles

properly. Most dogs are not picky eaters but, unless fed properly, can quickly succumb to skin problems.

enced breeders and trainers recommend crates as preferred tools for show puppies as well as pet puppies. Some breeders will only sell you a pup on the condition that you crate-train it.

Crates are not cruel—crates have many humane and highly effective uses in dog care and training. For example, crate training is a very popular and very successful housebreaking method. A crate can keep your dog safe during travel; and, perhaps most importantly, a crate provides your dog with a place of his own in

PHOTO COURTESY OF DOSKOCIL.

for your dog. Like his burrowing ancestors, he too will seek out the comfort and retreat of a den—you just happen to be providing him with something a little more luxurious than what his early ancestors enjoyed.

As far as purchasing a crate, the type that you buy is up to you. It will most likely be one of the two most popular types: wire or fiberglass. There are advantages and disadvantages to each type. For example, a wire crate is more open, allowing the air to flow through and affording the dog a view of what is going on around him, while a fiberglass crate is sturdier and less drafty. Both can double as travel crates, providing protection for the dog. A small crate will be sufficient to accommodate your Chihuahua.

INSURANCE

Just like you can insure your car, your house and your own health, you likewise can insure your dog's health. Investigate a pet insurance policy by talking to your vet. Depending on the age of your dog, the breed and the kind of coverage you desire, your policy can be very affordable. Most policies cover accidental injuries, poisoning and thousands of medical problems and illnesses. Some carriers also offer routine care and immunization coverage, including spaying/neutering, health screening and more.

Your local pet shop probably has a large variety of crates from which you can choose the one that best suits your needs.

your home. It serves as a "doggie bedroom" of sorts—your Chihuahua can curl up in his crate when he wants to sleep or when he just needs a break. Many dogs sleep in their crates overnight. When lined with soft bedding and with some of his favorite toys, a crate becomes a cozy pseudo-den

BEDDING

A soft mat in the dog's crate will help the dog feel more at home and you may also like to throw in a small blanket. This will take the place of the leaves, twigs, etc., that the pup would use in the wild to make a den; the pup can make his own burrow in the crate. Although your pup is far removed from his den-making ancestors, the denning instinct is still a part of his genetic makeup. Second, until you bring your pup home, he has been sleeping amid the warmth of his mother and littermates, and while a blanket is not the same as a warm, breathing body, it still provides heat and some-thing with which to snuggle. You will want to wash your pup's bedding frequently in case he has an accident in his crate, and replace or remove any blanket that becomes ragged and starts to fall apart.

TOYS

Toys are a must for dogs of all ages, especially for curious playful pups. Puppies are the "children" of the dog world, and what child does not love toys? Chew toys provide enjoyment to both dog and owner—your dog will enjoy playing with his favorite toys, while you will enjoy the fact that they distract him from your expensive shoes and leather couch. Puppies love

CRATE-TRAINING TIPS

Chihuahuas take to crates quite naturally and usually welcome the security and privacy that the crate provides. During crate training, you should partition off

the section of the crate in which the pup stays. If he is given too big an area, this will hinder your training efforts. Crate training is based on the fact that a dog does not like to soil his sleeping quarters, so it is ineffective to keep a pup in a crate that is so big that he can eliminate in one end and get far enough away from it to sleep.

Also, you want to make the crate den-like for the pup. Blankets and a favorite toy will make the crate cozy for the small pup. It will take some coaxing at first, but be patient. Given some time to get used to it, your pup will adapt to his new home-within-a-home quite nicely.

TOYS, TOYS, TOYS!

With a big variety of dog toys available, and so many that look like they would be a lot of fun for a dog, be careful in your selection. It is amazing what a set of puppy teeth

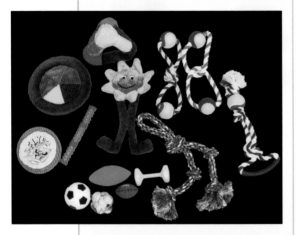

can do to an innocent-looking toy; so, obviously, safety is a major consideration. Be sure to choose the most durable products that you can find. Hard nylon bones and toys are a safe bet, and many of them are offered in different scents and flavors that will be sure to capture your dog's attention. It is always fun to play a game of fetch with your dog, and there are balls and flying discs that are specially made to withstand the wear-and-tear of dog teeth.

to chew; in fact, chewing is a physical need for pups as they are teething, and everything looks appetizing! The full range of your possessions—from old dish towel to Oriental carpet—are fair game in the eyes of a teething pup. Puppies are not all that discerning when it comes to finding something to literally "sink their teeth into"—everything tastes great!

Be careful of natural bones, which have a tendency to splinter into sharp, dangerous pieces. Also be careful of rawhide, which can turn into pieces that are easy to swallow and become a mushy mess on your carpet.

LEASH
A nylon leash is probably the best option as it is the most resistant to puppy teeth should your pup take a liking to chewing on his leash. Of course, this is a habit that should be nipped in the bud but, if your pup likes to chew on his leash, he has a very slim chance of being able to chew through the strong nylon. Nylon leashes are also lightweight, which is good for a Chihuahua who is just getting used to the idea of walking on a leash. For everyday walking and safety purposes, the nylon leash is a good choice. As your pup grows up and gets used to walking on the leash, you may want to purchase a flexible leash. These leashes allow you to extend the length to give the dog a broader area to explore or to shorten the

length to keep the dog closer to you. Of course, there are special show leads, and specially made halters or harnesses, which may be more comfortable for your Chihuahua.

COLLAR

Your pup should get used to wearing a collar all the time since you will want to attach his ID tags to it. Plus, you have to attach the leash to something! A lightweight nylon collar is a good choice; make sure that it fits snugly enough so that the pup cannot wriggle out of it, but is loose enough so that it will not be uncomfortably tight around the pup's neck. You should be able to fit a finger between the pup and the collar. It may take

Your local pet shop should have a wide variety of leashes from which you can select the lightest type for your Chihuahua.

some time for your pup to get used to wearing the collar, but soon he will not even notice that it is there.

FOOD AND WATER BOWLS

Your pup will need two bowls, one for food and one for water. You may want two sets of bowls, one for inside and one for outside, though your Chihuahua will not spend too much time outdoors. Stainless steel or sturdy plastic bowls are popular choices. Plastic bowls are more chewable. Dogs tend not to chew on the steel variety, which can be sterilized. It is important to buy sturdy bowls since anything is in danger of being chewed by puppy teeth and you do not want your dog to be constantly chewing his bowl (for his safety and for your wallet!).

FINANCIAL RESPONSIBILITY

Grooming tools, collars, leashes, a crate, a dog bed and, of course, toys will be expenses to you when you first obtain your pup, and the cost will continue throughout your dog's lifetime. If your puppy damages or destroys your possessions (as most puppies surely will!) or something belonging to a neighbor, you can calculate additional expense. There is also flea and pest control, which every dog owner faces more than once. You must be able to handle the financial responsibility of owning a dog.

CLEANING SUPPLIES

Until a pup is house-trained, you will be doing a lot of cleaning. "Accidents" will occur, which is all right in the beginning because the puppy does not know any better. All you can do is be prepared to clean up any accidents. Old rags, towels, newspapers and a safe disinfectant are good to have on hand.

BEYOND THE BASICS

The items previously discussed are the bare necessities. You will find out what else you need as you go along—grooming supplies, flea/tick protection, baby gates to partition a room, etc. These things will vary depending on your situation, but it is important that

you have everything you need to feed and make your Chihuahua comfortable in his first few days at home.

PUPPY-PROOFING YOUR HOME

Aside from making sure that your Chihuahua will be comfortable in your home, you also have to make sure that your home is safe for your Chihuahua. This means taking precautions that your pup will not get into anything he should not get into and that there is nothing within his reach that may harm him should he sniff it, chew it, inspect it, etc. This probably seems obvious since, while you are primarily concerned with your pup's safety,

All puppies, including Chihuahuas, love to chew on soft things. Offer only toys made for dogs, and monitor the condition of all of your ChiChi's toys, as soft toys are easily destructible.

at the same time you do not want your belongings to be ruined. Breakables should be placed out of reach if your dog is to have full run of the house. If he is to be limited to certain places within the house, keep any potentially dangerous items in the "off-limits" areas. An electrical cord can pose a danger should the puppy decide to taste it—and who is going to convince a pup that it would not make a great chew toy? Cords should be fastened tightly against the wall. If your dog is going to spend time in a crate, make sure that there is nothing near his crate that he can reach if he sticks his curious little nose or paws through the openings. Just as you would with a child, keep all household cleaners and chemicals where the pup cannot reach them.

It is also important to make sure that the outside of your home is safe. Of course your puppy should never be unsupervised, but a pup let loose in the yard will want to run and explore, and he should be granted that freedom. Do not let a fence give you a false sense of security; you would be surprised how crafty (and persistent) a dog can be in working out how to dig under and squeeze his way through small holes, or to climb over a fence. Be sure to repair or secure any gaps in the fence. Check the fence periodically to ensure that it is in good

BOY OR GIRL?

An important consideration to be discussed is the sex of your puppy. For a family companion, a bitch may be the better choice, considering the female's inbred concern for all young creatures and her accompanying tolerance and patience. It is always advisable to spay a pet bitch, which may guarantee her a longer life.

shape and make repairs as needed. A determined Chihuahua may return to the same spot to "work on it" until he is able to get through, and it doesn't take a terribly large hole for the Chihuahua to escape.

FIRST TRIP TO THE VET
You have picked out your puppy, and your home and family are ready. Now all you have to do is collect your Chihuahua from the breeder and the fun begins, right? Well…not so fast. Something else you need to prepare is your pup's first trip to the veterinarian. Perhaps the breeder can recommend someone in the area who specializes in Chihuahuas or toy breeds, or maybe you know some other Chihuahua owners who can suggest a good vet. Either way, you should have an appointment arranged for your pup before you pick him up and plan on taking him for an examination before bringing him home.

CHOOSE AN APPROPRIATE COLLAR

The BUCKLE COLLAR is the standard collar used for everyday purposes. Be sure that you adjust the buckle on growing puppies. Check it every day. It can become too tight overnight! These collars can be made of leather or nylon. Attach your dog's identification tags to this collar.

The CHOKE COLLAR is constructed of highly polished steel so that it slides easily through the stainless steel loop. The idea is that the dog controls the pressure around its neck and he will stop pulling if the collar becomes uncomfortable. Choke collars should *never* be used on a toy dog like the Chihuahua.

The HALTER is for a trained dog that has to be restrained to prevent running away, chasing a cat and the like. Considered the most humane of all restraining devices, it is frequently used on smaller dogs for which collars are not comfortable.

The pup's first visit will consist of an overall examination to make sure that the pup does not have any problems that are not apparent to you. The veterinarian will also set up a schedule for the pup's vaccinations; the breeder will inform you of which ones the pup has already received and the vet can continue from there.

INTRODUCTION TO THE FAMILY

Everyone in the house will be excited about the puppy's coming home and will want to pet him and play with him, but it is best to make the introduction low-key so as not to overwhelm the puppy. He is apprehensive already. It is the first time he has been separated from his mother and the breeder, and the ride to your home is likely to be the first time he has been in a car. The last thing you want to do is smother him, as this will only frighten him further. This is not to say that human contact is not extremely necessary at this stage, because this is the time when a connection between the pup and his human family is formed. Gentle petting and soothing words should help console him, as well as just putting him down and letting him explore on his own (under your watchful eye, of course).

HOW VACCINES WORK

If you've just bought a puppy, you surely know the importance of having your pup vaccinated, but do you understand how vaccines work?

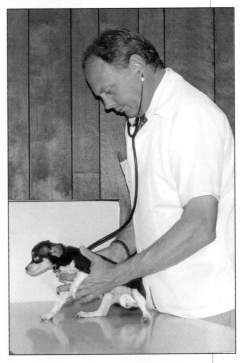

Vaccines contain the same bacteria or viruses that cause the disease you want to prevent, but they have been chemically modified so that they don't cause any harm. Instead, the vaccine causes your dog to produce antibodies that fight the harmful bacteria. Thus, if your pup is exposed to the disease in the future, the antibodies will destroy the viruses or bacteria. Discuss vaccinations with your veterinarian.

When purchasing bowls for your ChiChi, select small, shallow vessels. Your dog is going to eat and drink, not bathe in his bowl!

PHOTO COURTESY OF MIKKI PET PRODUCTS.

The pup may approach the family members or may busy himself with exploring for a while. Gradually, each person should spend some time with the pup, one at a time, crouching down to get as close to the pup's level as possible and letting him sniff their hands and petting him gently. He definitely needs human attention and he needs to be touched—this is how to form an immediate bond. Just remember that the pup is experiencing a lot of things for the first time, at the same time. There are new people, new noises, new smells and new things to investigate, so be gentle, be affectionate and be as comforting as you can be.

YOUR PUP'S FIRST NIGHT HOME

You have traveled home with your new charge safely in his basket or crate. He's been to the vet for a thorough check-up; he's been weighed, his papers examined; perhaps he's even been vaccinated and wormed as well. He's met the family and he's licked the whole family, including the excited children and the less-than-happy cat. He's explored his area, his new bed, the yard and anywhere else he's been permitted. He's eaten his first meal at home and relieved himself in the proper place. He's heard lots of new sounds, smelled new friends and seen more of the outside world than ever before.

That was just the first day! He's worn out and is ready for bed...or so you think!

It's puppy's first night and you are ready to say "Good night"—keep in mind that this is puppy's first night ever to be sleeping alone. His dam and littermates are no longer at paw's length and he's a bit scared, cold and lonely. Be reassuring to your new family member. This is not the time to spoil him and give in to his inevitable whining.

Puppies whine. They whine to let others know where they are and hopefully to get company out of it. Place your pup in his new bed or crate in his room and close the door. Mercifully, he may fall asleep without a peep. If the inevitable occurs, ignore the whining; he is fine. Be strong and keep his interest in mind. Do not allow yourself to feel guilty and visit the pup. He will fall asleep eventually.

Many breeders recommend placing a piece of bedding from his former home in his new bed so that he recognizes the scent of his littermates. Others still advise placing a hot water bottle in his bed for warmth. This latter may be a good idea provided the pup doesn't attempt to suckle—he'll get good and wet and may not fall asleep so fast.

Your local pet shop probably has tools that can make cleaning up more convenient.

Puppy's first night can be somewhat stressful for the pup and his new family. Remember that you are setting the tone of nighttime at your house. Unless you want to play with your pup every evening at 10 p.m., midnight and 2 a.m., don't initiate the habit. Your family will thank you, and so will your pup!

PREVENTING PUPPY PROBLEMS

SOCIALIZATION
Now that you have done all of the preparatory work and have helped your pup get accustomed to his new home and family, it is

TOXIC PLANTS

Many plants can be toxic to dogs. If you see your dog carrying a piece of vegetation in his mouth, approach him in a quiet, disinterested manner, avoid eye contact, pet him and gradually remove the plant from his mouth. Alternatively, offer him a treat and maybe he'll drop

the plant on his own accord. Be sure no toxic plants are growing in your own garden and that you have no toxic houseplants or flowers.

about time for you to have some fun! Socializing your Chihuahua pup gives you the opportunity to show off your new friend, and your pup gets to reap the benefits of being an adorable furry creature that people will want to pet and, in general, think is absolutely precious! It is wise for the new owner to realize that a Chihuahua held in his owner's arms is likely to be more defensive of his mistress than if he is walking on leash by her side. Let introductions be made from the ground or floor, without holding the pup in your arms.

Besides getting to know his new family, your puppy should be exposed to other people, animals and situations, but of course he must not come into close contact with dogs you don't know well until his course of injections is fully complete. This will help him become well adjusted as he grows up and less prone to being timid or fearful of the new things he will encounter. Be aware that larger dogs may not recognize your Chihuahua as "canine" and be aggressive. Be protective of your little charge, as some larger dogs may perceive him as prey.

Your pup's socialization began at the breeder's, but now it is your responsibility to continue it. The socialization he receives up until the age of 12 weeks is the most critical, as this is the time when he forms his impressions of the outside world. The eight-to-ten-week-old period is known as the fear period. Your pup will still be with the breeder during this time. The interaction he receives during this time should be gentle and reassuring. Lack of socialization can manifest itself in fear and aggression as the dog grows up. He needs lots of human contact, affection, handling and exposure to other animals.

Once your pup has received his necessary vaccinations, feel free to take him out and about (on his leash, of course). Walk him around the neighborhood, take him on your daily errands, let people pet him, let him meet other small dogs and pets, etc. Be wary of larger, aggressive dogs. Puppies do not have to try to make friends; there will be no shortage of people who will want to introduce themselves. Just make sure that you carefully supervise each meeting. If the neighborhood children want to say hello, for example, that is great—children and pups most often make great companions. Sometimes an excited child can unintentionally handle a pup too roughly, and although the Chihuahua is hardy, he is still a tiny thing and cannot endure any

rough handling. You want to make all socialization experiences positive ones. What a pup learns during this very formative stage will affect his attitude toward future encounters. You want your dog to be comfortable around everyone. A pup that has a bad experience with a child may grow up to be a dog that is shy around, fearful of or aggressive toward children.

CONSISTENCY IN TRAINING
Dogs, being pack animals, naturally need a leader, or else they try to establish dominance in their packs. When you bring a dog into your family, the choice of who becomes the leader and who becomes the "pack" is entirely up to you! Your pup's intuitive quest for dominance, coupled with the fact that it is nearly impossible to look at the palm-sized Chihuahua pup and not cave in, give the pup almost an unfair advantage in getting the upper hand! A pup will definitely test the waters to see what he can and cannot do. Do not give in to those pleading eyes—stand your ground when it comes to disciplining the pup and make sure that all family members do the same. Avoid discrepancies by having all members of the household decide on the rules before the pup even comes home…and be consistent in enforcing them! Early training

SOCIALIZATION

Thorough socialization includes not only meeting new people but also being introduced to new experiences such as riding in the car, having his coat brushed, hearing the television, walking in a crowd—the list is endless. The more your pup experiences, and the more positive the experiences are, the less of a shock and the less frightening it will be for your pup to encounter new things.

IN DUE TIME

It will take at least two weeks for your puppy to become accustomed to his new surroundings. Give him lots of love, attention, handling, frequent

opportunities to relieve himself, a diet he likes to eat and a place he can call his own.

shapes the dog's personality, so you cannot be unclear in what you expect.

COMMON PUPPY PROBLEMS

The best way to prevent puppy problems is to be proactive in stopping an undesirable behavior as soon as it starts. The old saying "You can't teach an old dog new tricks" does not necessarily hold true, but it is true that it is much easier to discourage bad behavior in a young developing pup than to wait until the pup's bad behavior becomes the adult dog's bad habit. There are some problems that are especially prevalent in puppies as they develop.

NIPPING
As puppies start to teethe, they feel the need to sink their teeth into anything available...unfortunately, that includes your fingers, arms, hair and toes. You may find this behavior cute for the first five seconds...until you feel just how sharp those puppy teeth are. This is something you want to discourage immediately and consistently with a firm "No!" (or whatever number of firm "Nos" it takes for him to understand that you mean business). Then replace your finger with an appropriate chew toy. Your Chihuahua does not mean any harm with a friendly nip, but he also does not know that his friendly nip can hurt.

CRYING/WHINING
Your pup will often cry, whine, whimper, howl or make some type of commotion when he is left alone. This is basically his way of calling out for attention to make sure that you know he is there and that you have not forgotten about him. He feels insecure when he is left alone,

when you are out of the house and he is in his crate or when you are in another part of the house and he cannot see you. The noise he is making is an expression of the anxiety he feels at being alone, so he needs to be taught that being alone is okay. You are not actually training the dog to stop making noise, you are training him to feel comfortable when he is alone and thus removing the need for him to make the noise. This is where the crate with cozy bedding and a toy comes in handy. You want to know that he is safe when you are not there to supervise, and you know that he will be safe in his crate rather than roaming freely about the house. In order for the pup to stay in his crate without making a fuss, he needs to be comfortable in his crate. On that note, it is extremely important that the crate is never used as a form of punishment, or the pup will have a negative association with the crate.

Accustom the pup to the crate in short, gradually increasing time intervals in which you put him in the crate, maybe with a treat, and stay in the room with him. If he cries or makes a fuss, do not go to him, but stay in his sight. Gradually he will realize that staying in his crate is all right without your help, and it will not be so

traumatic for him when you are not around. You may want to leave the radio on softly when you leave the house; the sound of human voices may be comforting to him.

CHEWING TIPS

Chewing goes hand in hand with nipping in the sense that a teething puppy is always looking for a way to soothe his aching gums. In this case, instead of chewing on you, he may have taken a liking to your favorite shoe or something else that he should not be chewing. Again, realize that this is a normal canine behavior that does not need to be discouraged, only redirected. Your pup just needs to be taught what is acceptable to chew on and what is off-limits. Consistently tell him NO when you catch him chewing on something forbidden and give him a chew toy.

Conversely, praise him when you catch him chewing on something appropriate. In this way, you are discouraging the inappropriate behavior and reinforcing the desired behavior. The puppy's chewing should stop after his adult teeth have come in, but an adult dog continues to chew for various reasons—perhaps because he is bored, needs to relieve tension or just likes to chew.

FEEDING YOUR CHIHUAHUA

NUTRITION

Today's high-quality dry premium foods are well formulated but are no more "complete" than types of breakfast cereal that claim to offer all the nutrition you need. You would not offer your child cereal three times a day, and you should not expect to raise a healthy dog only on that which comes to you attractively packaged in a bag.

It is a great leap of evolution to expect a species that only a flicker of time ago, gained sustenance from fresh fruits, berries, grasses, roots, mice, lizards, beetles and other small game suddenly to be transformed into a physiological package that prospers on a commercially prepared foodstuff. Entire books have been written on this subject but, suffice to say, you can measurably add to your Chihuahua's health and longevity by including fresh or raw food in his diet. Even if raised on standard kibble, he can quickly learn to appreciate apples, grapes or bananas. He will relish cooked chicken, raw chicken wings and small chunks of beef. Cooked carrots, broccoli and spinach also will be welcomed. In fact, the vegetables will reduce his need to eat grass.

Hard-boiled eggs, cottage cheese and yogurt are excellent natural sources of protein. If you

STORING DOG FOOD

You must store your dry dog food carefully. Open packages of dog food quickly lose their vitamin value, usually within 90 days of being opened. Mold spores and vermin could also contaminate the food.

can procure it, unpasteurized cow or goat milk will suit his digestive system better than the sterilized, pasteurized, homogenized form that you find in the grocery store. In actual fact, Nature did not intend for the adult canine to suckle milk past weaning, but a little treat will do no harm, especially if it is in the natural form.

During the weaning process, which lasts up to eight weeks, the puppy should have been fed four meals a day. By the time you adopt him at ten to twelve weeks, he can do quite nicely on three meals a day up to five or six months of age. He can then be fed twice a day, although our dogs are fed "wet" only once a day and have dry kibble for the second snack. The dry food can be skipped in favor of a good bone, which will serve the same purpose—nutrition and healthy exercise for teeth and gums.

MILK PRODUCTION

Milk production is the most elemental lesson in "supply and demand." The babies must suckle in order to stimulate the milk glands. Common sense will almost always ensure the beginnings of first-milk, which contains the colostrum necessary to stimulate the newborn immune system. Most new moms are either groggy from anesthesia, overwhelmed by the whole experience or just too

FOOD PREFERENCE

Selecting the best dry dog food is difficult. There is no majority consensus among veterinary scientists as to the value of nutrient analysis (protein, fat, fiber, moisture, ash, cholesterol, minerals, etc.). All agree that feeding trials are what matter, but you also have to consider the individual dog. The

dog's weight, age and activity level, and what pleases his taste, all must be considered. It is probably best to take the advice of your veterinarian. Every dog's dietary requirements vary, even during the lifetime of a particular dog.

Your Chihuahua can be fed a good dry food, along with portions of meat and/or vegetables. Chichis do appreciate variety in their diets. Consider adding some fruit or green vegetables to your dog's meals. You may also wish to add a little flavored stock to give a difference to the taste.

Chihuahua

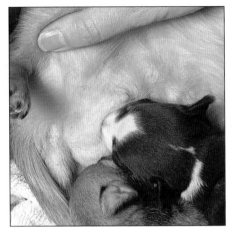

nervous to leave the nest to take in adequate liquid. The body's attempts to produce milk may lead to dehydration and things can go rapidly downhill.

For any situation in which the bitch refuses to drink adequate amounts of water, offer tidbits of baked ham. Ham or any type of fatty, salty real meat is usually quite irresistible to dogs and, as you well know, it stimulates thirst that lasts for several hours. Garlic is also a tasty treat that most dogs will relish and it too will cause a bitch to drink more. While powdered or granulated garlic will suffice in a pinch, a small clove sautéed in olive oil, then mashed in with a favorite food would be even better.

WATER

Just as your dog needs proper nutrition from his food, water is an essential "nutrient" as well. Water keeps the dog's body properly hydrated and promotes normal function of the body's systems. During housebreaking, it is necessary to keep an eye on how much water your Chihuahua is drinking, but once he is reliably trained he should have access to clean fresh water at all times, especially if you feed dry food. Make sure that the dog's water bowl is clean, and change the water often.

EXERCISE

Do not let the Chihuahua's small size mislead you—this is an

TREAT HIM LIKE A DOG

When fed a varied diet that includes raw bones, Chihuahuas maintain healthy teeth and gums and hopefully never see a vet for problems except for the rare surgical procedure. As regards overall health and hardiness, they are indeed "terrier-like" if they are not overly coddled. By all means, hold him, sleep with him, spoil him with a green bean from your plate, but allow him to be a dog! He will enjoy a raw bone just as much as the coyote enjoys his and for the same reasons. Gnawing a bone reduces stress and calms the soul of a dog. It will clean his teeth and stimulate both his gums and digestive track. Because he is so small, some otherwise intelligent humans lose the ability to reason and treat him like a stuffed toy instead of a highly evolved carnivore!

active dog that requires considerable exercise. Fortunately, the Chihuahua's legs are small and will not require a two-hour jog each day to stay in shape. Chihuahua owners tend to be more sedentary than their energetic dogs. These athletic dwarfs prefer to accompany their loved one on a daily walk, preferably for a mile or two. (In Greyhound steps, that's the equivalent of 50 or 60 miles!) For your sake, it's easier and shorter. A sedentary lifestyle is as harmful to a dog as it is to a person.

Regular walks, play sessions in the yard and letting the dog run free in a fenced area under your supervision make excellent exercise options for the Chihuahua. Obesity is a common problem for many dog breeds, especially toy breeds who enjoy being coddled and spoiled by their devoted owners. Bear in mind that an overweight dog should never be suddenly over-exercised; instead, he should be allowed to increase exercise slowly. Not only is exercise essential to keep the dog's body fit, it is essential to his mental well-being. A bored dog will find something to do, which often manifests itself in some type of destructive behavior. In this sense, exercise is essential for the owner's mental well-being as well!

BEATING THE "HO-HUM"

Your Chihuahua needs to stretch his legs and run before eating. The Chihuahua is more fortunate than large breeds confined inside, because nature designed the dog to engage in strenuous physical activity in order to secure the high-protein

food he needs. Wake him up, set down a bowl of dog food and any dog will go "ho-hum."

He also needs daily exercise in order to facilitate the elimination of waste. The inactivity forced upon large-breed house pets, combined with those awful stool-reducing prepared foods marketed today, keep dogs chronically constipated! And then we wonder why many confined dogs become lethargic, grumpy—or both!

GROOMING

COAT CARE AND BATHING

Bathing should occur about once a month. Although the breed sheds very little dander, he will collect dust and pollen due simply to being closer to the ground than most other dogs. He should be completely dried after a bath and kept indoors for a couple of hours afterward. If regularly bathed, he is virtually hypoallergenic.

In Longcoats, the ruff or furry part of the chest tends to become a bit more soiled, and if the dog should develop a loose stool, fecal matter can become stuck on the "pants." Hand-grooming (petting and stroking) keeps the coat glossy, but a rubber curry-comb made for small dogs will provide excellent stimulation for both skin and coat.

Eyes should be checked and wiped daily, especially after eating, so as to prevent staining. A little boric-acid solution or a product made especially for that purpose can be purchased from your vet. This will keep the face clean and attractive, and alert you

The eyes should be cleaned and checked on a daily basis. The tear stains can be easily removed with products on the market made especially for this purpose.

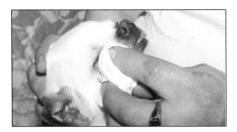

DRINK, DRANK, DRUNK— MAKE IT A DOUBLE

In both humans and dogs, as well as other living organisms, water forms the major part of nearly every body tissue. Naturally, we take water for granted, but without it, life as we know it would cease.

For dogs, water is needed to keep their bodies functioning biochemically. Additionally, water is needed to

replace the water lost while panting. Unlike humans, who are able to sweat to dissipate heat, dogs must pant to cool down, thereby losing the vital water that their bodies need to regulate their body temperatures. Humans lose electrolyte-containing products and other body-fluid components through sweating; dogs do not lose anything except water.

Water is essential always, but especially so when the weather is hot or humid or when your dog is exercising or working vigorously.

LET THE SUN SHINE

Your ChiChi worships the sun for good reason. Pets kept inside homes with curtains drawn against the sun

suffer from "SAD" (Seasonal Affected Disorder) to the same degree as humans. We now know that sunlight must enter the iris and thus progress to the pineal gland to regulate the body's hormonal system. When we live and work in artificial light, both circadian rhythms and hormone balances are disturbed.

your pup to being bathed as a puppy, it will be second nature by the time he grows up. You want your dog to be at ease in the bathtub or else it could end up a wet, soapy, messy ordeal for both of you!

Brush your Chihuahua thoroughly before wetting his coat. This will get rid of most mats and tangles (for Longcoats), which are harder to remove when the coat is wet. Make sure that your dog has a good non-slip surface to stand on. Begin by wetting the dog's coat. A shower or hose attachment may be necessary for thoroughly wetting and rinsing the coat. Check the water temperature to make sure that it is neither too hot nor too cold for *the dog.*

Next, apply shampoo to the dog's coat and work it into a good lather. You should purchase a shampoo that is made for dogs. Do not use a product made for human hair. Bathe the head last; you do not want shampoo to drip into the dog's eyes while you are washing the rest of his body. Work the shampoo all the way down to the skin. You can use this opportunity to check the skin for any bumps, bites or other abnormalities. Do not neglect any area of the body— get all of the hard-to-reach places.

Once the dog has been thoroughly shampooed, he requires an equally thorough rinsing. Shampoo left in the coat

to any possible problem or injury to the eye.

Regarding the bath, dogs do not need to be bathed as often as humans, but regular bathing is essential for healthy skin and a healthy, shiny coat. Again, like most anything, if you accustom

A daily brushing removes dead hairs and stimulates the skin.

The use of human soap products like shampoo, bubble bath and hand soap can be damaging to a dog's coat and skin. Human products are too strong; they remove the protective oils coating the dog's hair and skin that make him water-resistant. Use only shampoo made especially for dogs. You may like to use a medicated shampoo, which will help to keep external parasites at bay.

can be irritating to the skin. Protect his eyes from the shampoo by shielding them with your hand and directing the flow of water in the opposite direction. You should also avoid getting water in the ear canal. Be prepared for your dog to shake out his coat— you might want to stand back, but make sure you have a hold on the dog to keep him from running through the house.

Ear Cleaning

The ears should be kept clean and any excess hair inside the ear should be carefully plucked. Ears can be cleaned with a cotton ball and ear powder made especially for dogs, never probing into the

Ear cleaning should be done weekly. Excess hairs should be plucked (painless if done properly). Get instruction in ear care from your veterinarian.

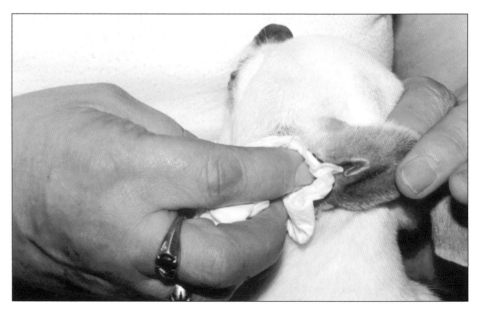

BATHING BEAUTY

Once you are sure that the dog is thoroughly rinsed, squeeze the excess water out of his coat with your hand and dry him with a heavy towel. You may choose to use a blow dryer on his coat or just let it dry naturally. In cold weather, never allow your dog outside with a wet coat.

There are "dry bath" products on the market, which are sprays and powders intended for spot cleaning that can be used between regular baths if necessary. They are not substitutes for regular baths, but they are easy to use for touch-ups as they do not require rinsing. Your pet shop should offer a selection of "dry bath" products.

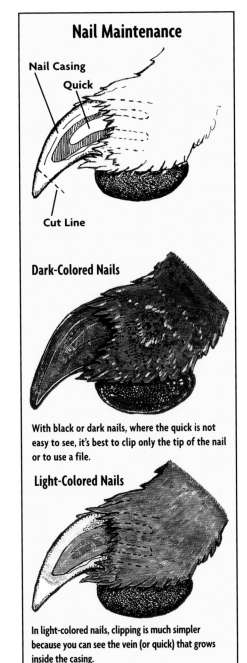

Nail Maintenance

Nail Casing

Quick

Cut Line

Dark-Colored Nails

With black or dark nails, where the quick is not easy to see, it's best to clip only the tip of the nail or to use a file.

Light-Colored Nails

In light-colored nails, clipping is much simpler because you can see the vein (or quick) that grows inside the casing.

ear canal. Be on the lookout for any signs of infection or ear-mite infestation. If your Chihuahua has been shaking his head or scratching at his ears frequently, this usually indicates a problem. If his ears have an unusual odor, this is a sure sign of mite infestation or infection, and a signal to have his ears checked by the veterinarian.

NAIL CLIPPING

Your Chihuahua should be accustomed to having his nails trimmed at an early age, since it will be part of your maintenance routine throughout his life. Not only does it look nicer, but long nails can be sharp and scratch

73

Your local pet shop sells proper clippers with which you can trim your dog's nails.

someone unintentionally. Also, a long nail has a better chance of ripping and bleeding, or causing damage to the toes. A good rule of thumb is that if you can hear your dog's nails' clicking on the floor when he walks, his nails are too long.

Before you start cutting, make sure you can identify the "quick" in each nail. The quick is a blood vessel that runs through the center of each nail and grows rather close to the end. It will bleed if accidentally cut, which will be quite painful for the dog as it contains nerve endings. Keep some type of clotting agent on hand, such as a styptic pencil or styptic powder (the type used for shaving). This will stop the bleeding quickly when applied to the end of the cut nail. Do not panic if this happens, just stop the bleeding and talk soothingly to your dog. Once he has calmed down, move on to the next nail. It is better to clip a little at a time, particularly with black-nailed dogs.

Hold your pup steady as you begin trimming his nails; you do

not want him to make any sudden movements or run away. Talk to him soothingly and stroke him as you clip. Holding his foot in your hand, simply take off the end of each nail in one quick clip. You can purchase nail clippers that are specially made for dogs; you can find them wherever you buy pet or grooming supplies.

TRAVELING WITH YOUR DOG

CAR TRAVEL
You should accustom your Chihuahua to riding in a car at an early age. You may or may not take him in the car often, but at the very least he will need to go to the vet and you do not want these trips to be traumatic for the dog or a big hassle for you. The safest way for a dog to ride in the car is in his crate. If he uses a crate in the

GOING ABROAD

For international travel, you will have to make arrangements well in advance (perhaps months), as countries' regulations pertaining to bringing in animals differ. There may be special health certificates and/or vaccinations that your dog will need before taking the trip; sometimes this has to be done within a certain time frame. When traveling to rabies-free countries, you will need to bring proof of the dog's rabies vaccination and there will likely be a quarantine period upon arrival.

house, you can use the same crate for travel.

Put the pup in the crate and see how he reacts. If he seems uneasy, you can have a passenger hold him on his lap while you drive. Another option is a specially made safety harness for dogs, which straps the dog in much like a seat belt. Do not let the dog roam loose in the vehicle—this is very dangerous! If you should stop short, your dog can be thrown and injured. If the dog starts climbing on you and pestering you while you are driving, you will not be able to concentrate on the road. It is an unsafe situation for everyone—human and canine.

For long trips, be prepared to stop to let the dog relieve himself. Bring along whatever you need to clean up after him. You should also take along some paper towels and perhaps some old rags for use should he have an accident in the car or suffer from motion sickness.

AIR TRAVEL

Every airline has different regulation and requirements for canine passengers. In most cases, the dog will be required to travel in a fiberglass crate but you should always check in advance with the airline regarding specific requirements. To help the dog be at ease, put one of his favorite toys in the crate with him. Do not feed the dog for several hours before checking in to minimize his need to relieve himself. However, certain regulations specify that water must always be made available to the dog in the crate.

Make sure that your dog is properly identified and that your contact information appears on his ID tags and on his crate. Likely, the airline will permit the Chihuahua to travel with his owner as a "carry-on," a distinct advantage to owning the smallest dog in the world. If the airline does not permit this privilege, you have two options: find another airline or leave your Chihuahua at home. Unlike many larger breeds, Chihuahuas are not suitable to travel as cargo. It is too risky for such a small dog.

The safest way for your Chihuahua to travel is in his crate.

TRAINING YOUR
CHIHUAHUA

Living with an untrained dog is a lot like owning a piano that you do not know how to play—it is a nice object to look at but it does not do much more than that to bring you pleasure. Now try taking piano lessons, and suddenly the piano comes alive and brings forth magical sounds and rhythms that set your heart singing and your body swaying.

The same is true with your Chihuahua. Any dog is a big responsibility and if not trained sensibly may develop unacceptable behavior that annoys you or could even cause family friction.

To train your Chihuahua, you may like to enroll in an obedience class. Teach him good manners as you learn how and why he behaves the way he does. Find out how to communicate with your dog and how to recognize and understand his communications with you. Suddenly the dog takes on a new role in your life—he is clever, interesting, well behaved and fun to be with. He demonstrates his bond of devotion to you daily. In other words, your Chihuahua does wonders for your ego because he constantly reminds you that you are not only his leader, you are his hero!

Those involved with teaching dog obedience and counseling owners about their dogs' behavior have discovered some interesting facts about dog ownership. For example, training dogs when they are puppies results in the highest rate of success in developing well-mannered and well-adjusted adult dogs. Training an older dog, from six months to six years of age, can produce almost equal results, providing that the owner accepts the dog's slower rate of learning capability and is willing to work patiently to help the dog succeed at developing to his fullest potential. Unfortunately, many owners of untrained adult dogs lack the patience factor, so they do not persist until their dogs are successful at learning particular behaviors.

Training a puppy aged 10 to 16 weeks (20 weeks at the most) is like working with a dry sponge in a pool of water. The pup soaks up whatever you show him and constantly looks for more things to do and learn. At this early age, his body is not yet producing hormones, and therein lies the reason for such a high rate of success. Without hormones, he is focused on his owners and not particularly interested in

HANDS OFF, AMIGO!

Although not the most threatening dog on the planet, your Chihuahua may be one of the most protective, especially when you are holding him safe in

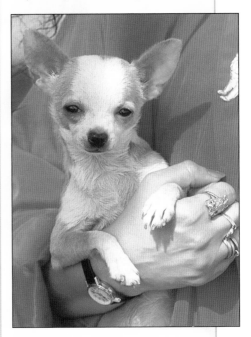

your arms. A Chihuahua who feels threatened by a friendly (grabbing) hand may quickly nip at his presumed assailant. This is an important factor to know before training begins, particularly if you are working with another handler.

investigating other places, dogs, people, etc. You are his leader: his provider of food, water, shelter and security. He latches onto you and wants to stay close. He will usually follow

77

however, you are hesitant or anxious about the approach of a stranger, he will respond accordingly.

Once the puppy begins to produce hormones, his natural curiosity emerges and he begins to investigate the world around him. It is at this time when you may notice that the untrained dog begins to wander away from you and even ignore your commands to stay close. When this behavior becomes a problem, the owner has two choices: get rid of the dog or train him. It is strongly urged that you choose the latter option.

There are usually classes within a reasonable distance from the owner's home, but you can also do a lot to train your dog yourself. Sometimes there are classes available but the tuition is too costly. Whatever the circumstances, the solution to the problem of training your

MEALTIME

Mealtime should be a peaceful time for your puppy. Do not put his food and water bowls in a high-traffic area in the house. For example, give him his own little corner of the kitchen where he can eat undisturbed and where he will not be underfoot. Do not allow small children or other family members to disturb the pup when he is eating.

The time and effort you devote to training the young dog will pay off for many years to come.

you from room to room, will not let you out of his sight when you are outdoors with him and will respond in like manner to the people and animals you encounter. If you greet a friend warmly, he will be happy to greet the person as well. If, dog without formal obedience lessons lies within the pages of this book.

This chapter is devoted to helping you train your Chihuahua at home. If the recommended procedures are followed faithfully, you may expect positive results that will prove rewarding both to you and your dog.

Whether your new charge is a puppy or a mature adult, the methods of teaching and the techniques we use in training basic behaviors are the same. After all, no dog, whether puppy or adult, likes harsh or inhumane methods. All creatures, however, respond favorably to gentle motivational methods and sincere praise and encouragement. Now let us get started.

HOUSEBREAKING

You can train a puppy to relieve himself wherever you choose, but this must be somewhere suitable. You should bear in mind from the outset that when your puppy is old enough to go out in public places, any canine deposits must be removed at once. You will always have to carry with you a small plastic bag or "poop-scoop."

Outdoor training includes such surfaces as grass, soil or dirt and cement. Indoor training usually means training your dog to newspaper.

CALM DOWN

Dogs will do anything for your attention. If you reward the dog when he is calm and attentive, you will develop a well-mannered dog.

If, on the other hand, you greet your dog excitedly and encourage him to wrestle with you, the dog will greet you the same way and you will have a hyperactive dog on your hands.

When deciding on the surface and location that you will want your Chihuahua to use, be sure it is going to be permanent. Training your dog to

79

By following the author's instructions, your puppy will be completely housebroken by the time his muscle and brain development reach maturity. Keep in mind that small breeds usually mature faster than large breeds, but all puppies should be trained by six months of age.

void. "Be quick" and "Hurry up" are examples of commands commonly used by dog owners.

Get in the habit of giving the puppy your chosen relief command before you take him out. That way, when he becomes an adult, you will be able to determine if he wants to go out when you ask him. A confirmation will be signs of interest, such as wagging his tail, watching you intently, going to the door, etc.

PUPPY'S NEEDS

Puppy needs to relieve himself after play periods, after each meal, after he has been sleeping and any time he indicates that he is looking for a place to urinate or defecate.

The urinary and intestinal tract muscles of very young puppies are not fully developed. Therefore, like human babies, puppies need to relieve themselves frequently.

Take your puppy out often— every hour for a ten-week-old, for example, and always immediately after sleeping and eating. The older the puppy, the less often he will need to relieve himself. Finally, as a mature healthy adult, he will require only three to five relief trips per day.

HOUSING

Since the types of housing and control you provide for your

grass and then changing your mind two months later is extremely difficult for both dog and owner.

Next, choose the command you will use each and every time you want your puppy to

CANINE DEVELOPMENT SCHEDULE

It is important to understand how and at what age a puppy develops into adulthood.
If you are a puppy owner, consult the following Canine Development Schedule to
determine the stage of development your puppy is currently experiencing.
This knowledge will help you as you work with the puppy in the weeks and months ahead.

Period	Age	Characteristics
FIRST TO THIRD	BIRTH TO SEVEN WEEKS	Puppy needs food, sleep and warmth, and responds to simple and gentle touching. Needs mother for security and disciplining. Needs littermates for learning and interacting with other dogs. Pup learns to function within a pack and learns pack order of dominance. Begin socializing with adults and children for short periods. Begins to become aware of its environment.
FOURTH	EIGHT TO TWELVE WEEKS	Brain is fully developed. Needs socializing with outside world. Remove from mother and littermates. Needs to change from canine pack to human pack. Human dominance necessary. Fear period occurs between 8 and 16 weeks. Avoid fright and pain.
FIFTH	THIRTEEN TO SIXTEEN WEEKS	Training and formal obedience should begin. Less association with other dogs, more with people, places, situations. Period will pass easily if you remember this is pup's change-to-adolescence time. Be firm and fair. Flight instinct prominent. Permissiveness and over-disciplining can do permanent damage. Praise for good behavior.
JUVENILE	FOUR TO EIGHT MONTHS	Another fear period about 7 to 8 months of age. It passes quickly, but be cautious of fright and pain. Sexual maturity reached. Dominant traits established. Dog should understand sit, down, come and stay by now.

NOTE: THESE ARE APPROXIMATE TIME FRAMES. ALLOW FOR INDIVIDUAL DIFFERENCES IN PUPPIES.

The crate becomes your Chihuahua's own special place in the home, aside from being a safe means of transport.

Instead, offer the puppy clearly defined areas where he can play, sleep, eat and live. A room of the house where the family gathers is the most obvious choice. Puppies are social animals and need to feel a part of the pack right from the start. Hearing your voice, watching you while you are doing things and smelling you nearby are all positive reinforcers that he is now a member of your pack. Usually a family room, the kitchen or a nearby adjoining breakfast area is ideal for providing safety and security for both puppy and owner.

Within that room, there should be a smaller area that the puppy can call his own. An alcove, a wire or fiberglass dog

puppy have a direct relationship on the success of housetraining, we consider the various aspects of both before we begin training.

Bringing a new puppy home and turning him loose in your house can be compared to turning a child loose in a sports arena and telling the child that the place is all his! The sheer enormity of the place would be too much for him to handle.

PAPER CAPER

Never line your pup's sleeping area with newspaper. Puppy litters are usually raised on newspaper and, once in your home, the puppy will immediately associate newspaper with voiding. Never put newspaper on any floor while house-training, as this will only confuse the puppy. If you are paper-training him, use paper in his designated relief area only. Finally, restrict water intake after evening meals. Offer a few licks at a time—never let a young puppy gulp water after meals.

crate or a fenced (not boarded!) corner from which he can view the activities of his new family will be fine. The size of the area or crate is the key factor here. The area must be large enough for the puppy to lie down and stretch out as well as stand up without rubbing his head on the top, yet small enough so that he cannot relieve himself at one end and sleep at the other without coming into contact with his droppings before he is fully trained to relieve himself outside.

Dogs are, by nature, clean animals and will not remain close to their relief areas unless forced to do so. In those cases, they then become dirty dogs and usually remain that way for life.

The designated area should be lined with clean bedding and a toy. Water must always be available, in a non-spill container, once house-training has been achieved reliably.

CONTROL

By control, we mean helping the puppy to create a lifestyle pattern that will be compatible to that of his human pack (you!). Just as we guide little children to learn our way of life, we must show the puppy when it is time to play, eat, sleep, exercise and even entertain himself.

Your puppy should always

TAKE THE LEASH

Do not carry your dog to his relief area. Lead him there on a leash or, better yet, encourage him to follow you to the spot. If you start carrying him to his spot, you might end up doing this routine forever and your dog will have the satisfaction of having trained *you*.

sleep in his crate. He should also learn that, during times of household confusion and excessive human activity, such as at breakfast when family members are preparing for the day, he can play by himself in relative safety and comfort in his designated area. Each time you leave the puppy alone, he should understand exactly where he is to stay. Puppies are chewers. They cannot tell the difference between lamp cords, television wires, shoes, table legs, etc. Chewing into a television wire, for example, can be fatal to the puppy, while a shorted wire can start a fire in the house.

If the puppy chews on the arm of the chair when he is alone, you will probably discipline him angrily when you get home. Thus, he makes the association that your coming home means he is going to be punished. (He will not remember chewing on the chair and is incapable of making the association of the discipline with his naughty deed.)

Other times of excitement, such as family parties, etc., can be fun for the puppy, providing he can view the activities from the security of his designated area. He is not underfoot and he is not being fed all sorts of tidbits that will probably cause him stomach distress, yet he still feels a part of the fun.

SCHEDULE

A puppy should be taken to his relief area each time he is released from his designated area, after meals, after a play

> ## HOW MANY TIMES A DAY?
>
> | AGE | RELIEF TRIPS |
> |-----|-------------|
> | To 14 weeks | 10 |
> | 14–22 weeks | 8 |
> | 22–32 weeks | 6 |
> | Adulthood | 4 |
> | (dog stops growing) | |
>
> These are estimates, of course, but they are a guide to the minimum number of opportunities a dog should have each day to relieve himself.

session and when he first awakens in the morning (at age ten weeks, this can mean 5 a.m.!). The puppy will indicate that he's ready "to go" by circling or sniffing busily—do not misinterpret these signs. For a puppy less than 12 weeks of age, a routine of taking him out every hour is necessary. As the puppy grows, he will be able to wait for longer periods of time.

Keep trips to his relief area short. Stay no more than five or six minutes and then return to the house. If he goes during that time, praise him lavishly and take him indoors immediately. If he does not, but he has an accident when you go back indoors, pick him up immediately, say "No! No!" and return to his relief area. Wait a few minutes, then return to the house again. Never hit a puppy or put his face in urine or excrement when he has had an accident!

Once indoors, put the puppy in his crate until you have had time to clean up his accident. Then release him to the family area and watch him more closely than before. Chances are, his accident was a result of your not picking up his signal or waiting too long before offering him the opportunity to relieve himself. Never hold a grudge against the puppy for accidents.

Let the puppy learn that going outdoors means it is time to relieve himself, not play. Once trained, he will be able to

THE SUCCESS METHOD

Success that comes by luck is usually short-lived. Success that comes by well-thought-out proven methods is often more easily achieved and permanent. This is the Success Method. It is designed to give you, the puppy owner, a simple yet proven way to help your puppy develop clean living habits and a feeling of security in his new environment.

6 Steps to Successful Crate Training

1 Tell the puppy "Crate time!" and place him in the crate with a small treat (a piece of cheese or half of a biscuit). Let him stay in the crate for five minutes while you are in the same room. Then release him and praise lavishly. Never release him when he is fussing. Wait until he is quiet before you let him out.

2 Repeat Step 1 several times a day.

3 The next day, place the puppy in the crate as before. Let him stay there for ten minutes. Do this several times.

4 Continue building time in five-minute increments until the puppy stays in his crate for 30 minutes with you in the room. Always take him to his relief area after prolonged periods in his crate.

5 Now go back to Step 1 and let the puppy stay in his crate for five minutes, this time while you are out of the room.

6 Once again, build crate time in five-minute increments with you out of the room. When the puppy will stay willingly in his crate (he may even fall asleep!) for 30 minutes with you out of the room, he will be ready to stay in it for several hours at a time.

your activities. Let him learn that having you near is comforting, but it is not your main purpose in life to provide him with undivided attention.

Each time you put a puppy in his own area, use the same command, whatever suits best. Soon he will run to his crate or special area when he hears you say those words.

Crate training provides safety for you, the puppy and the home. It also provides the puppy with a feeling of security, and that helps the puppy achieve self-confidence and clean habits.

Remember that one of the primary ingredients in house-training your puppy is control. Regardless of your lifestyle, there will always be occasions when you will need to have a

THE CLEAN LIFE

By providing sleeping and resting quarters that fit the dog, and offering frequent opportunities to relieve himself outside his quarters, the puppy quickly learns that the outdoors (or the newspaper if you are training him to paper) is the place to go when he needs to urinate or defecate. It also reinforces his innate desire to keep his sleeping quarters clean. This, in turn, helps develop the muscle control that will eventually produce a housebroken dog with clean living habits.

Training and exhibiting build confidence in your Chihuahua. This breed thrives on structure and praise.

play indoors and out and still differentiate between the times for play versus the times for relief.

Help him develop regular hours for naps, being alone, playing by himself and just resting, all in his crate. Encourage him to entertain himself while you are busy with

THE GOLDEN RULE

The golden rule of dog training is simple. For each "question" (command), there is only one correct answer (reaction). One command = one reaction. Keep practicing the command until the dog reacts correctly without hesitating. Be repetitive but not monotonous. Dogs get bored just as people do!

place where your dog can stay and be happy and safe. Crate training is the answer for now and in the future.

In conclusion, a few key elements are really all you need for a successful house-training method—consistency, frequency, praise, control and supervision. By following these procedures with a normal, healthy puppy, you and the puppy will soon be past the stage of "accidents" and ready to move on to a full and rewarding life together.

ROLES OF DISCIPLINE, REWARD AND PUNISHMENT

Discipline, training one to act in accordance with rules, brings order to life. It is as simple as that. Without discipline, particularly in a group society, chaos reigns supreme and the group will eventually perish. Humans and canines are social animals and need some form of discipline in order to function

effectively. They must procure food, protect their home base and their young and reproduce to keep the species going.

If there were no discipline in the lives of social animals, they would eventually die from starvation and/or predation by other stronger animals. In the case of domestic canines, dogs need discipline in their lives in order to understand how their pack (you and other family members) functions and how they must act in order to survive.

A large humane society in a highly populated area recently surveyed dog owners regarding their satisfaction with their relationships with their dogs. People who had trained their dogs were 75% more satisfied with their pets than those who had never trained their dogs.

Dr. Edward Thorndike, a psychologist, established *Thorndike's Theory of Learning*,

Developing a loving rapport with your Chihuahua will make training a snap. This is one smart little dog that lives to please you.

RULES TO OBEY

If you want to be successful in training your dog, you have four rules to obey yourself:

1. Develop an understanding of how a dog thinks.
2. Do not blame the dog for lack of communication.
3. Define your dog's personality and act accordingly.
4. Have patience and be consistent.

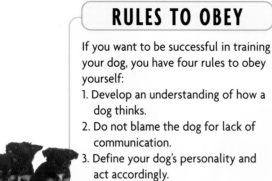

which states that a behavior that results in a pleasant event tends to be repeated. A behavior that results in an unpleasant event tends not to be repeated. It is this theory on which training methods are based today. For example, if you manipulate a dog to perform a specific behavior and reward him for doing it, he is likely to do it again because he enjoyed the end result.

Occasionally, punishment, a penalty inflicted for an offense, is necessary. The best type of punishment often comes from an outside source. For example, a child is told not to touch the stove because he may get burned. He disobeys and touches the stove. In doing so, he receives a burn. From that time on, he respects the heat of the stove and avoids contact with it. Therefore, a behavior that results

in an unpleasant event tends not to be repeated.

A good example of a dog learning the hard way is the dog who chases the house cat. He is told many times to leave the cat alone, yet he persists in teasing the cat. Then, one day he begins chasing the cat but the cat turns and swipes a claw across the dog's face, leaving him with a painful gash on his nose. The final result is that the dog stops chasing the cat.

TRAINING EQUIPMENT

COLLAR AND LEASH

For a Chihuahua, the collar and leash that you use for training must be one with which you are easily able to work, not too heavy for the dog and perfectly safe.

TREATS

Have a bag of treats on hand. Something nutritious and easy to swallow works best. Use a soft treat, a small chunk of cheese or a piece of cooked chicken rather than a dry biscuit. By the time the dog has finished chewing a dry treat, he will forget why he is being rewarded in the first place! Using food rewards will not teach a dog to beg at the table— the only way to teach a dog to beg at the table is to give him food from the table. In training,

KEEP SMILING

Never train your dog, puppy or adult, when you are angry or in a sour mood. Dogs are very sensitive to human feelings, especially anger, and if your dog senses that you are angry or upset, he will connect your anger with his training and learn to resent or fear his training sessions.

rewarding the dog with a food treat will help him associate praise and the treats with learning new behaviors that obviously please his owner.

TRAINING BEGINS: ASK THE DOG A QUESTION

In order to teach your dog anything, you must first get his attention. After all, he cannot

Training your dog begins with practice, rewards and praise. If you have any dreams of actually showing your dog, start show training as early as possible.

HONOR AND OBEY

Dogs are the most honorable animals in existence. They consider another species (humans) as their own. You are their leader and they look to you for guidance and proper care. With such a tiny breed, young children must be supervised at all times, and everyone should handle the dog with care.

learn anything if he is looking away from you with his mind on something else.

To get his attention, ask him "School?" and immediately walk over to him and give him a treat as you tell him "Good dog." Wait a minute or two and repeat the routine, this time with a treat in your hand as you approach within a foot of the dog. Do not go directly to him, but stop about a foot short of him and hold out the treat as you ask "School?" He will see you approaching with a treat in your hand and most likely begin walking toward you. As you meet, give him the treat and praise again.

The third time, ask the question, have a treat in your hand and walk only a short distance toward the dog so that he must walk almost all the way to you. As he reaches you, give him the treat and praise again.

By this time, the dog will probably be getting the idea that if he pays attention to you, especially when you ask that question, it will pay off in treats and enjoyable activities for him. In other words, he learns that "school" means doing fun things with you that result in treats and positive attention for him.

Remember that the dog does not understand your verbal language; he only recognizes sounds. Your question translates to a series of sounds for him, and those sounds become the signal to go to you and pay attention.

THE BASIC COMMANDS

TEACHING SIT

Now that you have the dog's attention, attach his leash and hold it in your left hand and a food treat in your right. Place your food hand at the dog's nose and let him lick the treat but not take it from you. Say "Sit" and slowly raise your food hand from in front of the dog's nose up over his head so that he is looking up. As he bends his head upward, he will have to bend his knees to maintain his balance. As he bends his knees, he will assume a sit position. At that point, release the food treat and praise lavishly with comments such as "Good dog! Good sit!," etc. Remember to always praise enthusiastically, because dogs relish verbal praise from their owners and feel so proud of themselves whenever they accomplish a behavior.

You will not use food forever in getting the dog to obey your commands. Food is only used to teach new behaviors, and once the dog knows what you want when you give a specific command, you will wean him off the food treats but still maintain the verbal

THINK BEFORE YOU BARK!

Dogs are sensitive to their masters' moods and emotions. Use your voice wisely when communicating with your dog. Never raise your voice at your dog unless you are trying to correct him; do not shout when giving commands. "Barking" at your dog can become as meaning-less as "dogspeak" is to you.

LANGUAGE BARRIER

Dogs do not understand our language. They can be trained to react to a certain sound, at a certain volume. If you say "No, Oliver" in a very soft, pleasant voice, it will not have the same meaning as "No, Oliver!!" when

you speak loudly. You should never use the dog's name during a reprimand, just the command "No!"

Since dogs don't understand words, comics often train dogs to commands with opposite meaning. Thus, when the comic commands his dog to sit, the dog will stand up, and vice versa.

praise. After all, you will always have your voice with you, and there will be many times when you have no food rewards but expect the dog to obey.

TEACHING DOWN

Teaching the down exercise is easy when you understand how the dog perceives the down position, and it is very difficult when you do not. Dogs perceive the down position as a submissive one, therefore teaching the down exercise using a forceful method can sometimes make the dog develop such a fear of the down that he either runs away when you say "Down" or he attempts to snap at the person who tries to force him down.

Have the dog sit close alongside your left leg, facing in the same direction as you are. Hold the leash in your left hand and a food treat in your right. Now place your left hand lightly on the top of the dog's shoulders where they meet above the spinal cord. Do not push down on the dog's shoulders; simply rest your left hand there so you can guide the dog to lie down close to your left leg rather than to swing away from your side when he drops.

Now place the food hand at the dog's nose, say "Down" very softly (almost a whisper), and slowly lower the food hand to the dog's front feet. When the food hand reaches the floor, begin moving it forward along the floor in front of the dog. Keep talking softly to the dog, saying things like, "Do you want this treat? You can do this, good dog." Your reassuring tone of voice will help calm the dog as he tries to follow the food hand in order to get the treat.

When the dog's elbows touch the floor, release the food and praise softly. Try to get the dog to maintain that down position for several seconds before you let him sit up again. The goal here is to get the dog to settle down and not feel threatened in the down position.

TEACHING STAY

It is easy to teach the dog to stay in either a sit or a down position. Again, we use food and praise during the teaching process as we help the dog to understand exactly what it is that we are expecting him to do.

To teach the sit/stay, start with the dog sitting on your left side as before and hold the leash in your left hand. Have a food treat in your right hand and place your food hand at the dog's nose. Say "Stay" and step out on your right foot to stand directly in front of the dog, toe to toe, as he licks and nibbles the treat. Be sure to keep his head facing upward to maintain the sit position. Count to five

DOUBLE JEOPARDY

A dog in jeopardy never lies down. He stays alert on his feet because instinct tells him that he may have to run away or fight for his survival. Therefore, if a dog feels threatened or anxious, he will not lie down. Consequently, it is important to keep the dog calm and relaxed as he learns the down exercise.

and then swing around to stand next to the dog again with him on your left. As soon as you get back to the original position, release the food and praise lavishly.

To teach the down/stay, do the down as previously described. As soon as the dog lies down, say "Stay" and step out on your right foot just as you did in the sit/stay. Count to five and then return to stand beside the dog with him on your left side. Release the treat and praise as always.

Within a week or ten days, you can begin to add a bit of distance between you and your dog when you leave him. When you do, use your left hand open with the palm facing the dog as a stay signal, much the same as the hand signal a police officer uses to stop traffic at an intersection. Hold the food treat in your right hand as before, but this time the food is not touching the dog's nose. He will watch the food hand and quickly learn that he is going to get that treat as soon as you return to his side.

When you can stand 1 yard away from your dog for 30 seconds, you can then begin building time and distance in both stays. Eventually, the dog can be expected to remain in the stay position for prolonged periods of time until you return to him or call him to you.

Always praise lavishly when he stays.

TEACHING COME

If you make teaching "come" an enjoyable experience, you should never have a "student" that does not love the game or that fails to come when called. The secret, it seems, is never to teach the word "come."

At times when an owner most wants his dog to come when called, the owner is likely upset or anxious and he allows these feelings to come through in the tone of his voice when he calls his dog. Hearing that desperation in his owner's voice, the dog fears the results of going to him and therefore either disobeys outright or runs in the opposite direction. The secret, therefore, is to teach the dog a game and, when you want him to come to you, simply play the game. It is practically a no-fail solution!

To begin, have several members of your family take a few food treats and each go into a different room in the house. Take turns calling the dog, and each person should celebrate the dog's finding him with a treat and lots of happy praise. When a person calls the dog, he is actually inviting the dog to find him and get a treat as a reward for "winning."

A few turns of the "Where

CONSISTENCY PAYS OFF

Dogs need consistency in their feeding schedule, exercise and relief visits, and in the verbal commands you use. If you use "Stay" on Monday

and "Stay here, please" on Tuesday, you will confuse your dog. Don't demand perfect behavior during training sessions and then let him have the run of the house the rest of the day. Above all, lavish praise on your pet consistently every time he does something right. The more he feels he is pleasing you, the more willing he will be to learn.

95

SAFETY FIRST

While it may seem that the most important things to your dog are eating, sleeping and chewing the upholstery on your furniture, his first concern is actually safety. The domesticated dogs we keep as

companions have the same pack instinct as their ancestors who ran free thousands of years ago. Because of this pack instinct, your dog wants to know that he and his pack are not in danger of being harmed, and that his pack has a strong, capable leader. You must establish yourself as the leader early on in your relationship. That way, your dog will trust that you will take care of him and the pack, and he will accept your commands without question.

are you?" game and the dog will understand that everyone is playing the game and that each person has a big celebration awaiting his success at locating them. Once he learns to love the game, simply calling out "Where are you?" will bring him running from wherever he is when he hears that all-important question.

The come command is recognized as one of the most important things to teach a dog, but there are trainers who work with thousands of dogs and never teach the actual word "come." Yet these dogs will race to respond to a person who uses the dog's name followed by "Where are you?" For example, a woman has a 12-year-old companion dog who went blind, but who never fails to locate her owner when asked, "Where are you?"

Children, in particular, love to play this game with their dogs. Children can hide in smaller places like a shower or bathtub, behind a bed or under a table. The dog needs to work a little bit harder to find these hiding places but, when he does, he loves to celebrate with a treat and a tussle with a favorite youngster.

TEACHING HEEL

Heeling means that the dog walks beside the owner without pulling. It takes time and patience on the owner's part to succeed at teaching the dog that he (the owner) will not proceed unless the dog is walking calmly beside him. Pulling out ahead on the leash is definitely not acceptable.

Begin by holding the leash in your left hand as the dog sits beside your left leg. Move the loop end of the leash to your right hand but keep your left hand short on the leash so it keeps the dog in close next to you.

Say "Heel" and step forward on your left foot. Keep the dog close to you and take three steps. Stop and have the dog sit next to you in what we now call the heel position. Praise verbally, but do not touch the dog. Hesitate a moment and begin again with "Heel," taking three steps and stopping, at which point the dog is told to sit again.

Your goal here is to have the dog walk those three steps without pulling on the leash. When he will walk calmly beside you for three steps without pulling, increase the number of steps you take to five. When he will walk politely beside you while you take five steps, you can increase the length of your walk to ten steps. Keep increasing the length of your stroll until the dog will walk quietly beside you without pulling as long as you want him

FEAR AGGRESSION

Pups who are subjected to physical abuse during training commonly end up with behavioral problems as adults. One common result of abuse is fear aggression, in which a dog will lash out, bare his teeth, snarl and finally bite someone by whom he feels threatened. For example, your daughter may be playing with the dog one afternoon. As they play hide-and-seek, she backs the dog into a corner and, as she attempts to tease him playfully, he bites her hand. Examine the cause of this behavior. Did your daughter ever hit the dog? Did someone who resembles your daughter hit or scream at the dog?

Fortunately, fear aggression is relatively easy to correct. Have your daughter engage in only positive activities with the dog, such as feeding, petting and walking. She should not give any corrections or negative feedback. If the dog still growls or cowers away from her, allow someone else to accompany them. Soon, the dog should feel confident that he can trust her and rely on her for many positive things, and he will also be prevented from reacting fearfully towards anyone who might resemble her.

to heel. When you stop heeling, indicate to the dog that the exercise is over by verbally praising as you pet him and say "OK, good dog." The "OK" is

HELPING PAWS

Your dog may not be the next Lassie, but every pet has the potential to do some tricks well. Identify his natural talents and hone them. Is your dog always happy and upbeat? Teach him to

wag his tail or give you his paw on command. Real homebodies can be trained to do household chores, such as picking up his toys or carrying a stray sock.

used as a release word, meaning that the exercise is finished and the dog is free to relax.

If you are dealing with a dog who insists on pulling ahead, simply "put on your brakes" and stand your ground until the dog realizes that the two of you are not going anywhere until he is beside you and moving at your pace, not his. It may take some time just standing there to convince the dog that you are the leader and you will be the one to decide on the direction and speed of your travel.

Each time the dog looks up at you or slows down to give a slack leash between the two of you, quietly praise him and say, "Good heel. Good dog." Eventually, the dog will begin to respond and within a few days he will be walking politely beside you without pulling on the leash. At first, the training sessions should be kept short and very positive; soon the dog will be able to walk nicely with you for increasingly longer distances. Remember also to give the dog free time and the opportunity to run and play when you have finished heel practice.

WEANING OFF FOOD IN TRAINING
Food is used in training new behaviors. Once the dog understands what behavior goes with a specific command, it is

Do not overwhelm
your Chihuahua
with overly long
lessons or too
many new
experiences in the
same day.

time to start weaning him off the
food treats. At first, give a treat
after each exercise. Then, start to
give a treat only after every other
exercise. Mix up the times when
you offer a food reward and the
times when you only offer praise
so that the dog will never know
when he is going to receive both
food and praise and when he is

THE STUDENT'S STRESS TEST

During training sessions, you must be able to recognize signs of stress in your dog
such as:

- tucking his tail between his legs
- lowering his head
- shivering or trembling
- standing completely still
  or running away
- panting and/or salivating

- avoiding eye contact
- flattening his ears back
- urinating submissively
- rolling over and lifting a leg
- grinning or baring teeth
- aggression when restrained

If your four-legged student displays these signs, he may just be nervous or intimidated. The training session may have been too lengthy, with not enough praise and
affirmation. Stop for the day and try again tomorrow.

Chihuahua

A BORN PRODIGY

Occasionally, a dog and owner who have not attended formal classes have been able to earn entry-level titles by obtaining competition rules and regulations from a local kennel club and practicing on their own to a degree of perfection. Obtaining the higher level titles, however, almost always requires extensive training under the tutelage of experienced instructors. In addition, the more difficult levels require more special-ized equipment whereas the lower levels do not.

At obedience trials, dogs can earn titles at various levels of competition. The beginning levels of competition include basic behaviors such as sit, down, heel, etc. The more advanced levels of competition include jumping, retrieving, scent discrimination and signal work. The advanced levels require a dog and owner to put a lot of time and effort into their training and the titles that can be earned at these levels of competition are very prestigious.

Every Chihuahua is an individual. Train your dog by following your good instincts about what methods work and which methods do not. Devise your own lesson plan based on your Chihuahua's strengths and abilities.

going to receive only praise. This is called a variable ratio reward system and it proves successful because there is always the chance that the owner will produce a treat, so the dog never stops trying for that reward. No matter what, *always* give verbal praise.

OBEDIENCE CLASSES

It is a good idea to enroll in an obedience class if one is available in your area. If yours is a show dog, showing classes would be more appropriate. Many areas have dog clubs that offer basic obedience training as well as preparatory classes for obedience competition. There are also local dog trainers who offer similar classes.

101

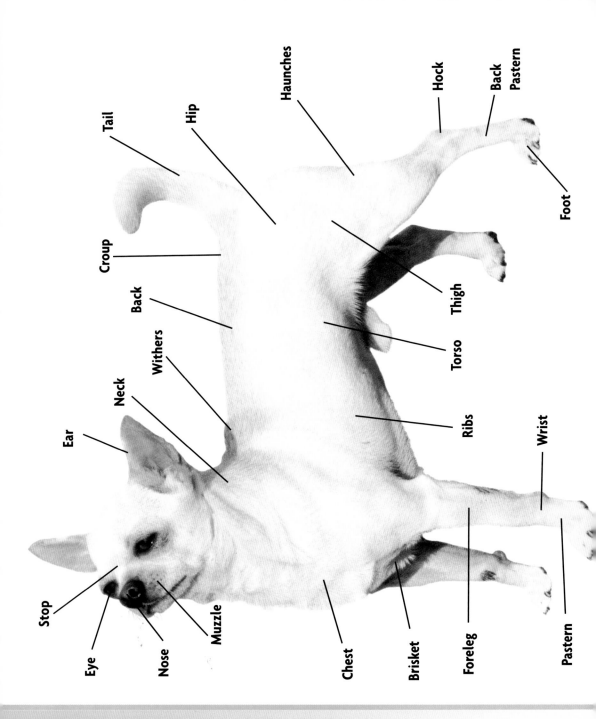

Physical Structure of the Chihuahua

Haunches
Hock
Back
Pastern
Tail
Hip
Foot
Croup
Thigh
Back
Withers
Neck
Torso
Ear
Ribs
Wrist
Stop
Eye
Nose
Muzzle
Chest
Brisket
Foreleg
Pastern

CHIHUAHUA

Dogs suffer from many of the same physical illnesses as people. They might even share many of the same psychological problems. Since people usually know more about human diseases than canine maladies, many of the terms used in this chapter will be familiar but not necessarily those used by veterinarians. We will use the term *x-ray*, instead of the more acceptable term *radiograph*. We will also use the familiar term *symptoms* even though dogs don't have symptoms, which are verbal descriptions of the patient's feelings; dogs have *clinical signs*. Since dogs can't speak, we have to look for clinical signs...but we still use the term *symptoms* in this book.

As a general rule, medicine is *practiced*. That term is not arbitrary. Medicine is a

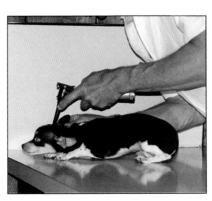

constantly changing art as we learn more and more about genetics, electronic aids (like CAT scans and MRIs) and daily laboratory advances. There are many dog maladies, like canine hip dysplasia, which are not universally treated in the same manner. Some veterinarians opt for surgery more often than others do.

SELECTING A QUALIFIED VETERINARIAN

Your selection of a veterinarian should be based not only upon personality and ability but also upon his convenience to your home. You require a veterinarian who is close because you might have emergencies or need to make multiple visits for treatments. You require a vet who has services that you might require such as tattooing

The vet is your dog's best friend! Routine veterinary check-ups are the best preventative medicine.

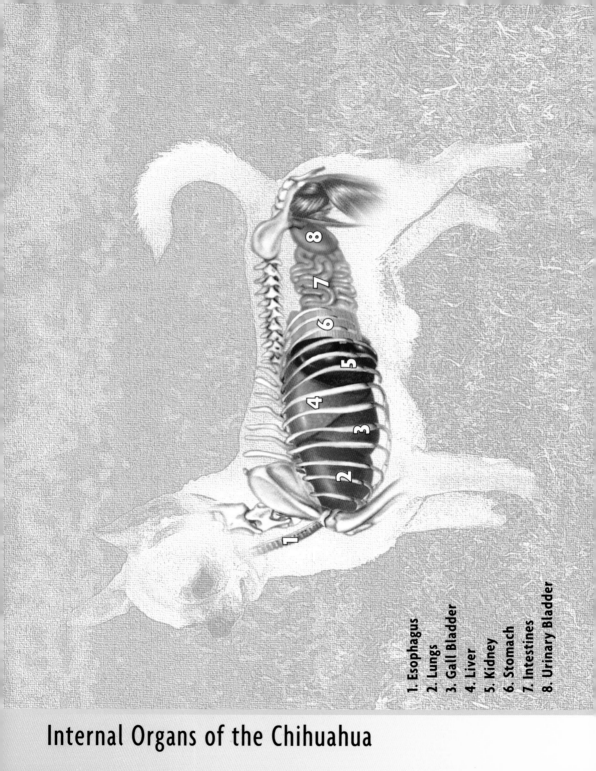

1. Esophagus
2. Lungs
3. Gall Bladder
4. Liver
5. Kidney
6. Stomach
7. Intestines
8. Urinary Bladder

Internal Organs of the Chihuahua

and boarding, as well as sophisticated pet supplies and a good reputation for ability and responsiveness. There is nothing more frustrating than having to wait a day or more to get a response from your veterinarian. You should seek a vet who has experience with the Chihuahua (or at least with toy breeds) since when a Chihuahua begins to fail, it can do so very rapidly and there may not be time for second guessing.

All veterinarians are licensed and their diplomas and/or certificates should be displayed in their waiting rooms. There are, however, many veterinary specialties that usually require further studies and internships. There are specialists in heart problems (veterinary cardiologists), skin problems (veterinary dermatologists), teeth and gum problems (veterinary dentists), eye problems (veterinary ophthalmologists) and x-rays (veterinary radiologists), as well as

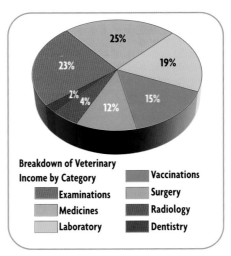

Breakdown of Veterinary Income by Category

- Examinations
- Medicines
- Laboratory
- Vaccinations
- Surgery
- Radiology
- Dentistry

A typical vet's income, categorized according to services provided. This survey dealt with small-animal practices.

surgeons who have specialties in bones, muscles or other organs. Most veterinarians do routine surgery such as neutering, stitching up wounds and docking tails for those breeds in which such is required for show purposes.

When the problem affecting your dog is serious, it is not unusual or impudent to get another medical opinion, although it is courteous to advise the vets concerned about this. You might also want to compare costs among several veterinarians. Sophisticated health care and veterinary services can be very costly. Don't be bashful about discussing these costs with your veterinarian or his staff. Important decisions are often based upon financial considerations.

NEUTERING/SPAYING

Males are castrated. The operation removes both testicles. Recovery takes about one week. Females are spayed; in this operation, the uterus (womb) and both of the ovaries are removed. This is major surgery and recovery takes about two weeks.

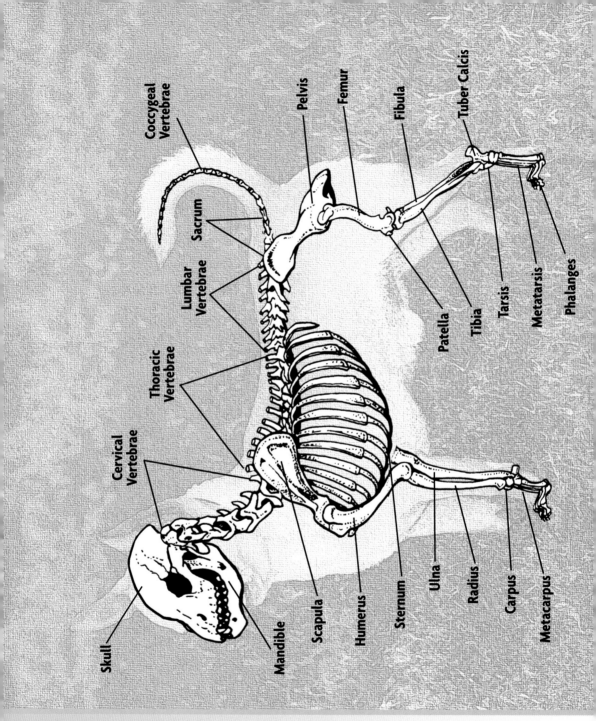

Coccygeal Vertebrae

Pelvis

Femur

Fibula

Tuber Calcis

Sacrum

Lumbar Vertebrae

Thoracic Vertebrae

Cervical Vertebrae

Patella

Tibia

Tarsis

Metatarsis

Phalanges

Skull

Mandible

Scapula

Humerus

Sternum

Ulna

Radius

Carpus

Metacarpus

Skeletal Structure of the Chihuahua

PREVENTATIVE MEDICINE

It is much easier, less costly and more effective to practice preventative medicine than to fight bouts of illness and disease. Properly bred puppies come from parents that were selected based upon their genetic disease profiles. The mother should have been vaccinated, free of all internal and external parasites, and properly nourished. For these reasons, a visit to the veterinarian who cared for the dam is recommended. The dam can pass on disease resistance to her puppies, which can last for eight to ten weeks. She can also pass on parasites and many infections. That's why you should find out as much as possible about the dam.

VACCINATION SCHEDULING

Most vaccinations are given by injection and should only be done by a veterinarian. Both he and you should keep a record of the date of the injection, the identification of the vaccine and the amount given. Some vets give a first vaccination at six to eight weeks, but most dog breeders prefer the course not to commence until about ten weeks because of negating any antibodies passed on by the dam. The vaccination scheduling is usually based on a 15-day cycle. You must take

KNOW WHEN TO POSTPONE A VACCINATION

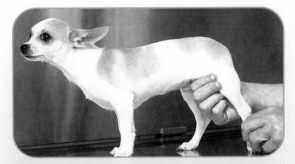

While the visit to the vet is costly, it is never advisable to update a vaccination when visiting with a sick or pregnant dog. Vaccinations should be avoided for all elderly dogs. If your dog is showing the signs of any illness or any medical condition, no matter how serious or mild, including skin irritations, do not vaccinate. Likewise, a lame dog should never be vaccinated; any dog undergoing surgery or on any immunosuppressant drugs should not be vaccinated until fully recovered.

your vet's advice as to when to vaccinate as this may differ according to the vaccine used. Most vaccinations immunize your puppy against viruses.

The usual vaccines contain immunizing doses of several different viruses such as distemper, parvovirus, parainfluenza and hepatitis. There are other vaccines available when the puppy is at risk. You should rely upon professional advice. This is especially true for the booster-shot program. Most vaccination programs require a

VACCINE ALLERGIES

Vaccines do not work all the time. Sometimes dogs are allergic to them and many times the antibodies, which are supposed to be stimulated by the vaccine, just are not produced. You should keep your dog in the veterinary clinic for an hour after he is vaccinated to be sure there are no allergic reactions.

booster when the puppy is a year old and once a year thereafter. In some cases, circumstances may require less frequent immunizations; discuss this prospect with your vet.

Canine cough, more formally known as tracheobronchitis, is treated with a vaccine that is sprayed into the dog's nostrils. Canine cough is usually included in routine vaccination, but it is often not as effective as those for other major diseases.

WEANING TO FIVE MONTHS OLD
Puppies should be weaned by the time they are about two months old. A puppy that remains for at least eight weeks with its mother and littermates usually adapts better to other dogs and people later in its life.

Some new owners have their puppy examined by a veterinarian immediately, which is a good idea. Vaccination

programs usually begin when the puppy is very young.

The puppy will have its teeth examined and have its skeletal conformation and general health checked prior to certification by the veterinarian. Puppies in certain breeds have problems with their kneecaps, cataracts and other eye problems, heart murmurs and undescended testicles. They may also have personality problems and your veterinarian might have training in temperament evaluation.

FIVE MONTHS TO ONE YEAR OF AGE
Unless you intend to breed or show your dog, neutering the puppy at six months of age is recommended. Discuss this with your veterinarian; most professionals advise neutering (males) and spaying (females). This has proven to be extremely beneficial to both male and female puppies. Besides eliminating the possibility of pregnancy, it inhibits (but does not prevent) breast cancer in bitches and prostate cancer in male dogs. Under no circumstances should a bitch be spayed prior to her first season.

Your veterinarian should provide your puppy with a thorough dental evaluation at six months of age, ascertaining whether all permanent teeth have erupted properly. A home dental-care regimen should be initiated at six months, including brushing weekly and providing good dental devices. Regular dental care promotes healthy teeth and fresh breath.

OVER ONE YEAR OF AGE

Once a year, your grown dog should visit the vet for an examination and vaccination boosters. Some vets recommend blood tests, thyroid-level check and dental evaluation to accompany these annual visits. A thorough clinical evaluation by the veterinarian can provide critical background information for your dog. Blood tests are often performed at one year of

KEEP OFF THE LAWN

Dogs who have been exposed to lawns sprayed with herbicides have double and triple the rate of malignant lymphoma. Suburban dogs are especially at risk, as they are exposed to lawns and gardens. Dogs perspire and absorb through their footpads. Be careful where your dog walks and always avoid any area that appears yellowed from chemical overspray.

age, and dental examinations around the third or fourth birthday. In the long run, quality preventative care for your pet can save money, teeth and lives.

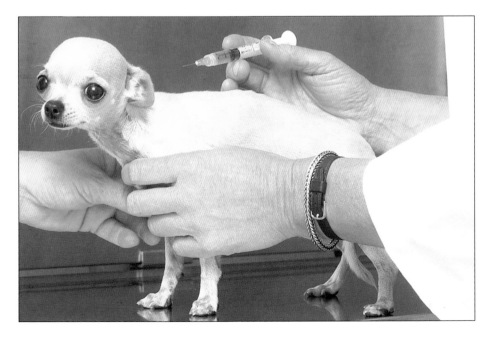

Every dog should be vaccinated by a veterinarian. It is important that injections be scheduled and administered at the appropriate times.

HEALTH AND VACCINATION SCHEDULE

Age in Weeks:	6TH	8TH	10TH	12TH	14TH	16TH	20-24TH	52ND
Worm Control	✔	✔	✔	✔	✔	✔	✔	
Neutering								✔
Heartworm		✔		✔		✔	✔	
Parvovirus	✔		✔		✔		✔	✔
Distemper		✔		✔		✔		✔
Hepatitis		✔		✔		✔		✔
Leptospirosis								✔
Parainfluenza	✔		✔		✔			✔
Dental Examination		✔					✔	✔
Complete Physical		✔					✔	✔
Coronavirus				✔			✔	✔
Canine Cough	✔							
Hip Dysplasia								✔
Rabies							✔	

Vaccinations are not instantly effective. It takes about two weeks for the dog's immune system to develop antibodies. Most vaccinations require booster shots. Your veterinarian should guide you in this regard.

SKIN PROBLEMS

Veterinarians are consulted by dog owners for skin problems more than any other group of diseases or maladies. Dogs' skin is almost as sensitive as human skin and both suffer almost the same ailments. (Though the occurrence of acne in most breeds of dog is rare!) For this reason, veterinary dermatology has developed into a specialty practiced by many veterinarians.

Since many skin problems have visual symptoms that are almost identical, it requires the skill of an experienced veterinary dermatologist to identify and cure many of the more severe skin disorders. Pet shops sell many treatments for skin problems, but most of the treatments are directed at symptoms and not the underlying problem(s). If your dog is suffering from a skin disorder, you should seek professional assistance as quickly as possible. As with all diseases, the earlier a problem is identified and treated, the better the chances for a complete recovery.

HEREDITARY SKIN DISORDERS

Veterinary dermatologists are currently researching a number of skin disorders that are believed to have a hereditary basis. These inherited diseases are transmitted by both parents, who appear (phenotypically) normal but have a recessive gene for the disease, meaning that they carry, but are not affected by, the disease. These diseases pose serious problems to breeders because in some instances there is no method of identifying carriers. Often the secondary diseases associated with these skin conditions are even more debilitating than the skin disorder, including cancers and respiratory problems.

Among the known hereditary skin disorders, for which the mode of inheritance is known, are acrodermatitis, cutaneous asthenia (Ehlers-Danlos syndrome), sebaceous adenitis, cyclic hematopoiesis, dermatomyositis, IgA deficiency, color dilution alopecia and nodular

DISEASE REFERENCE CHART

	What is it?	What causes it?	Symptoms
Leptospirosis	Severe disease that affects the internal organs; can be spread to people.	A bacterium, which is often carried by rodents, that enters through mucus membranes and spreads quickly throughout the body.	Range from fever, vomiting and loss of appetite in less severe cases to shock, irreversible kidney damage and possibly death in most severe cases.
Rabies	Potentially deadly virus that infects warm-blooded mammals.	Bite from a carrier of the virus, mainly wild animals.	1st stage: dog exhibits change in behavior, fear. 2nd stage: dog's behavior becomes more aggressive. 3rd stage: loss of coordination, trouble with bodily functions.
Parvovirus	Highly contagious virus, potentially deadly.	Ingestion of the virus, which is usually spread through the feces of infected dogs.	Most common: severe diarrhea. Also vomiting, fatigue, lack of appetite.
Canine cough	Contagious respiratory infection.	Combination of types of bacteria and virus. Most common: *Bordetella bronchiseptica* bacteria and parainfluenza virus.	Chronic cough.
Distemper	Disease primarily affecting respiratory and nervous system.	Virus that is related to the human measles virus.	Mild symptoms such as fever, lack of appetite and mucus secretion progress to evidence of brain damage, "hard pad."
Hepatitis	Virus primarily affecting the liver.	Canine adenovirus type I (CAV-1). Enters system when dog breathes in particles.	Lesser symptoms include listlessness, diarrhea, vomiting. More severe symptoms include "blue-eye" (clumps of virus in eye).
Coronavirus	Virus resulting in digestive problems.	Virus is spread through infected dog's feces.	Stomach upset evidenced by lack of appetite, vomiting, diarrhea.

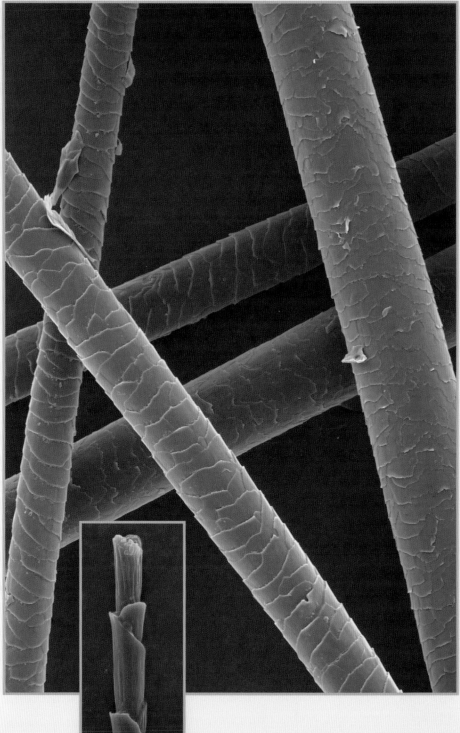

Normal hairs of a dog enlarged 200 times original size. The cuticle (outer covering) is clean and healthy. Unlike human hair that grows from the base, a dog's hair also grows from the end, as shown in the inset.

dermatofibrosis. Some of these disorders are limited to one or two breeds and others affect a large number of breeds. All inherited diseases must be diagnosed and treated by a veterinary specialist.

PARASITE BITES

Many of us are allergic to insect bites. The bites itch, erupt and may even become infected. Dogs have the same reaction to fleas, ticks and/or mites. When an insect lands on you, you have the chance to whisk it away with your hand. Unfortunately, when our dog is bitten by a flea, tick or mite, it can only scratch it away or bite it. By the time the dog has been bitten, the parasite has done some of its damage. It may also have laid eggs to cause further problems in the near future. The itching from parasite bites is probably due to the saliva injected into the site when the parasite sucks the dog's blood.

AUTO-IMMUNE SKIN CONDITIONS

Auto-immune skin conditions are commonly referred to as being allergic to yourself, while allergies are usually inflammatory reactions to outside stimuli. Auto-immune diseases cause serious damage to the tissues that are involved.

The best known auto-immune disease is lupus,

A SKUNKY PROBLEM

Have you noticed your dog dragging his rump along the floor? If so, it is likely that his anal sacs are impacted or possibly infected. The anal sacs are small pouches located on both sides of the anus under the skin and muscles. They are about the size and shape of a grape and contain a foul-smelling liquid. Their contents are usually emptied when the dog has a bowel movement but, if not emptied

completely, they will impact, which will cause your dog much pain. Fortunately, your veterinarian can tend to this problem easily by draining the sacs for the dog. Be aware that your dog might also empty his anal sacs in cases of extreme fright.

which affects people as well as dogs. The symptoms are variable and may affect the kidneys, bones, blood chemistry and skin. It can be fatal to both dogs and humans, though it is not thought to be transmissible. It is usually successfully treated with cortisone, prednisone or a similar corticosteroid, but extensive use of these drugs can have harmful side effects.

PUPPY VACCINATIONS

Your veterinarian will probably recommend that your puppy be fully vaccinated before you take him outside. There are airborne diseases, parasite eggs in the grass and unexpected visits from other dogs that might be dangerous to your puppy's health.

AIRBORNE ALLERGIES

Just as humans have hay fever, rose fever and other fevers from which they suffer during the pollinating season, many dogs suffer from the same allergies. When the pollen count is high, your dog might suffer, but don't expect him to sneeze and have a runny nose like a human would. Dogs react to pollen allergies the same way they react to fleas—they scratch and bite themselves.

Dogs, like humans, can be tested for allergens. Discuss the testing with a qualified veterinary dermatologist.

FOOD PROBLEMS

FOOD ALLERGIES

Dogs are allergic to many foods that are best-sellers and highly recommended by breeders and veterinarians. Changing the brand of food that you buy may not eliminate the problem if the element to which the dog is allergic is contained in the new brand.

Recognizing a food allergy

First Aid at a Glance

Burns
Place the affected area under cool water; use ice if only a small area is burnt.

Bee stings/Insect bites
Apply ice to relieve swelling; antihistamine dosed properly.

Animal bites
Clean any bleeding area; apply pressure until bleeding subsides; go to the vet.

Spider bites
Use cold compress and a pressurized pack to inhibit venom's spreading.

Antifreeze poisoning
Induce vomiting with hydrogen peroxide. Seek *immediate* veterinary help!

Fish hooks
Removal best handled by vet; hook must be cut in order to remove.

Snake bites
Pack ice around bite; contact vet quickly; identify snake for proper antivenin.

Car accident
Move dog from roadway with blanket; seek veterinary aid.

Shock
Calm the dog, keep him warm; seek immediate veterinary help.

Nosebleed
Apply cold compress to the nose; apply pressure to any visible abrasion.

Bleeding
Apply pressure above the area; treat wound by applying a cotton pack.

Heat stroke
Submerge dog in cold bath; cool down with fresh air and water; go to the vet.

Frostbite/Hypothermia
Warm the dog with a warm bath, electric blankets or hot water bottles.

Abrasions
Clean the wound and wash out thoroughly with fresh water; apply antiseptic.

Remember: an injured dog may attempt to bite a helping hand from fear and confusion. Always muzzle the dog before trying to offer assistance.

FOOD INTOLERANCE

Food intolerance is the inability of the dog to completely digest certain foods. For example, puppies that may have done very well on their mother's milk may not do well on cow's milk. The result of this food intolerance may be loose bowels, passing gas and stomach pains. These are the only obvious symptoms of food intolerance and that makes diagnosis difficult.

TREATING FOOD PROBLEMS

It is possible to handle food allergies and food intolerance yourself. Put your Chihuahua on a diet that he has never had. Obviously, if he has never eaten this new food, he can't have been allergic or intolerant of it. Start with a single

Feeding your dog properly is very important. An incorrect diet could affect the dog's health, behavior and nervous system. Its most visible effects are to the skin and coat.

is difficult. Humans vomit or have rashes when they eat a food to which they are allergic. Dogs neither vomit nor (usually) develop a rash. They react in the same manner as they do to an airborne or flea allergy; they itch, scratch and bite. This makes the diagnosis extremely difficult. While pollen allergies are usually seasonal, food allergies are year-round problems.

CARETAKER OF TEETH

You are your dog's caretaker and his dentist. Vets warn that plaque and tartar buildup on the teeth will damage the gums and allow bacteria to enter the dog's bloodstream, causing serious damage to the animal's vital organs. Studies show that over 50 percent of dogs have some form of gum disease before age three. Daily or weekly tooth cleaning (with a canine toothbrush or soft gauze pad wipes) can add to your dog's life.

ingredient that is not in the dog's diet at the present time. Ingredients like chopped beef or chicken are common in dogs' diets, so try something more exotic like rabbit, pheasant or another protein source. Keep the dog on this diet (with no additives) for a month. If the symptoms of food allergy or intolerance disappear, chances are your dog has a food allergy.

Don't think that the single ingredient cured the problem. You still must find a suitable diet and ascertain which ingredient in the old diet was objectionable. This is most easily done by adding ingredients to the new diet one at a time. Let the dog stay on the modified diet for a month before you add another ingredient. Eventually, you will determine the ingredient that caused the adverse reaction.

An alternative method is to carefully study the ingredients in the diet to which your Chihuahua is allergic or intolerant. Identify the main ingredient in this diet and eliminate the main ingredient by buying a different food that does not have that ingredient. Keep experimenting this way until the symptoms disappear after at least one month on the new diet.

DENTAL HEALTH

A dental examination is in order when the dog is between six months and one year of age so that any permanent teeth that have erupted incorrectly can be corrected. It is important to begin a brushing routine at home with your Chihuahua and to remain faithful to

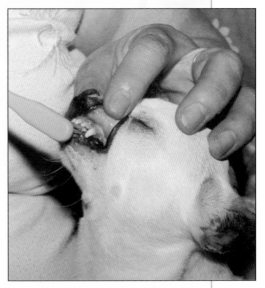

it. Toy dogs are known for their inferior teeth and bites, so care is ever so vital. Durable nylon and safe edible chews should be part of your puppy's arsenal for good health, good teeth and pleasant breath. The vast majority of dogs three to four years old and older has diseases of the gums from lack of dental attention. Using the various types of dental chews can be very effective in controlling dental plaque.

A male dog flea,
Ctenocephalides
canis.

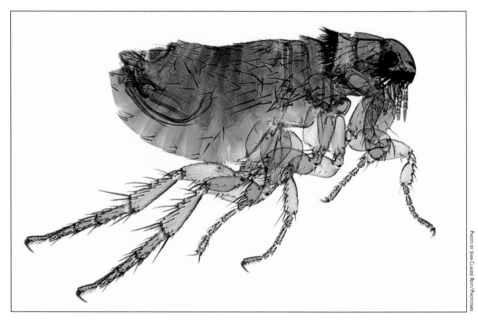

PHOTO BY JEAN CLAUDE REVY/PHOTOTAKE

EXTERNAL PARASITES

FLEAS
Of all the problems to which dogs are prone, none is more well known and frustrating than fleas. Flea infestation is relatively simple to cure but difficult to prevent. Parasites that are harbored inside the body are a bit more difficult to eradicate but they are easier to control.

To control flea infestation, you have to understand the flea's life cycle. Fleas are often thought of as a summertime problem, but centrally heated homes have changed the patterns and fleas can be found at any time of the year. The most effective method of flea control is a two-stage approach: one stage to kill the adult fleas, and the other to control the development of pre-adult fleas. Unfortunately, no single active ingredient is effective against all stages of the life cycle.

FLEA KILLER CAUTION– "POISON"

Flea-killers are poisonous. You should not spray these toxic chemicals on areas of a dog's body that he licks, including his genitals and his face. Flea killers taken internally are a better answer, but check with your vet in case internal therapy is not advised for your dog.

LIFE CYCLE STAGES

During its life, a flea will pass through four life stages: egg, larva, pupa or nymph and adult. The adult stage is the most visible and irritating stage of the flea life cycle, and this is why the majority of flea-control products concentrate on this stage. The fact is that adult fleas account for only 1% of the total flea population, and the other 99% exist in pre-adult stages, i.e., eggs, larvae and nymphs. The pre-adult stages are barely visible to the naked eye.

THE LIFE CYCLE OF THE FLEA

Eggs are laid on the dog, usually in quantities of about 20 or 30, several times a day. The adult female flea must have a blood meal before each egg-laying session. When first laid, the eggs will cling to the dog's hair, as the eggs are still moist. However, they will quickly dry out and fall from the dog, especially if the dog moves around or scratches. Many eggs will fall off in the dog's favorite area or an area in which he spends a lot of time, such as his bed.

Once the eggs fall from the dog onto the carpet or furniture, they will hatch into larvae. This takes from one to ten days. Larvae are not particularly mobile and will usually travel only a few inches from where they hatch. However, they do have a tendency to move away from

EN GARDE: CATCHING FLEAS OFF GUARD!

Consider the following ways to arm yourself against fleas:

- Add a small amount of pennyroyal or eucalyptus oil to your dog's bath. These natural remedies repel fleas.
- Supplement your dog's food with fresh garlic (minced or grated) and a hearty amount of brewer's yeast, both of which ward off fleas.
- Use a flea comb on your dog daily. Submerge fleas in a cup of bleach to kill them quickly.
- Confine the dog to only a few rooms to limit the spread of fleas in the home.
- Vacuum daily...and get all of the crevices! Dispose of the bag every few days until the problem is under control.
- Wash your dog's bedding daily. Cover cushions where your dog sleeps with towels, and wash the towels often.

bright light and heavy traffic—under furniture and behind doors are common places to find high quantities of flea larvae.

The flea larvae feed on dead organic matter, including adult flea feces, until they are ready to change into adult fleas. Fleas will usually remain as larvae for around seven days. After this period, the larvae will pupate

Photo by Dwight R. Kuhn.

Fleas have been measured as being able to jump 300,000 times and can jump over 150 times their length in any direction, including straight up.

into protective pupae. While inside the pupae, the larvae will undergo metamorphosis and change into adult fleas. This can take as little time as a few days, but the adult fleas can remain inside the pupae waiting to hatch for up to two years. The pupae are signaled to hatch by certain stimuli, such as physical pressure—the pupae's being stepped on, heat from an animal's lying on the pupae or increased carbon-dioxide levels and vibrations—indicating that a suitable host is available.

Once hatched, the adult flea must feed within a few days. Once the adult flea finds a host, it

will not leave voluntarily. It only becomes dislodged by grooming or the host animal's scratching. The adult flea will remain on the host for the duration of its life unless forcibly removed.

TREATING THE ENVIRONMENT AND THE DOG

Treating fleas should be a two-pronged attack. First, the environment needs to be treated; this includes carpets and furniture, especially the dog's bedding and areas underneath furniture. The environment should be treated with a household spray containing an Insect Growth Regulator (IGR) and an insecticide to kill the adult fleas. Most IGRs are effective against eggs and larvae; they actually mimic the fleas' own hormones and stop the eggs and larvae from developing into adult fleas. There are currently no treatments available to attack the pupa stage of the life cycle, so the adult insecticide is used to kill the newly hatched adult fleas before they find a host. Most IGRs are active for many months, while adult insecticides are only active for a few days.

A scanning electron micrograph of a dog or cat flea, Ctenocephalides, magnified more than 100x. This image has been colorized for effect.

S. E. M. by Dr. Dennis Kunkel, University of Hawaii.

THE LIFE CYCLE OF THE FLEA

Adult

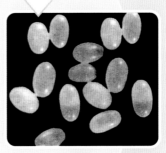

Egg

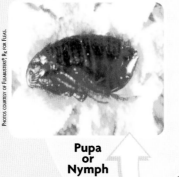

**Pupa
or
Nymph**

Larva

Fleas have been around for millions of years and have adapted to changing host animals. They are able to go through a complete life cycle in less than one month or they can extend their lives to almost two years by remaining as pupae or cocoons. They do not need blood or any other food for up to 20 months.

THE IGR

Two types of products should be used when treating fleas—a product to treat the pet and a product to treat the home. Adult fleas represent less than 1% of the flea population. The pre-adult fleas (eggs, larvae and pupae) represent more than 99% of the flea population and are found in the environment; it is in the case of pre-adult fleas that products containing an Insect Growth Regulator (IGR) should be used in the home.

IGRs are a new class of compounds used to prevent the development of insects. They do not kill the insect outright, but instead use the insect's biology against it to stop it from completing its growth. Products that contain methoprene are the world's first and leading IGRs. Used to control fleas and other insects, this type of IGR will stop flea larvae from developing and protect the house for up to seven months.

The American dog tick, Dermacentor variabilis, is probably the most common tick found on dogs. Look at the strength in its eight legs! No wonder it's hard to detach them.

When treating with a household spray, it is a good idea to vacuum before applying the product. This stimulates as many pupae as possible to hatch into adult fleas. The vacuum cleaner should also be treated with an insecticide to prevent the eggs and larvae that have been collected in the vacuum bag from hatching.

The second stage of treatment is to apply an adult insecticide to the dog. Traditionally, this would be in the form of a collar or a spray, but more recent innovations include digestible insecticides that poison the fleas when they ingest the dog's blood. Alternatively, there are drops that, when placed on the back of the dog's neck, spread throughout the hair and skin to kill adult fleas.

TICKS
Though not as common as fleas, ticks are found all over the tropical and temperate world. They don't bite, like fleas; they harpoon. They dig their sharp proboscis (nose) into the dog's skin and drink the blood. Their only food and drink is dog's

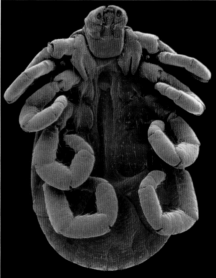

S. E. M. BY DR. DENNIS KUNKEL, UNIVERSITY OF HAWAII.

blood. Dogs can get Lyme disease, Rocky Mountain spotted fever, tick bite paralysis and many other diseases from ticks. They may live where fleas are found and they like to hide in cracks or seams in walls. They are controlled the same way fleas are controlled.

The American dog tick, *Dermacentor variabilis*, may well be the most common dog tick in many geographical areas, especially those areas where the climate is hot and humid. Most dog ticks have life expectancies of a week to six months, depending upon climatic conditions. They can neither jump nor fly, but they can crawl slowly and can range up to 16 feet to reach a sleeping or unsuspecting dog.

MITES

Just as fleas and ticks can be problematic for your dog, mites can also lead to an itchy nuisance. Microscopic in size, mites are related to ticks and generally take up permanent residence on their host animal— in this case, your dog! The term *mange* refers to any infestation caused by one of the mighty mites, of which there are six varieties that concern dog owners.

Demodex mites cause a condition known as demodicosis (sometimes called red mange or follicular mange), in which the

DEER-TICK CROSSING

The great outdoors may be fun for your dog, but it also is a home to dangerous ticks. Deer ticks carry a bacterium known as *Borrelia burgdorferi* and are most active in the autumn and spring. When infections are caught early, penicillin and tetracycline are effective antibiotics, but, if left untreated, the bacteria may cause neurological, kidney and cardiac problems as well as long-term trouble with walking and painful joints.

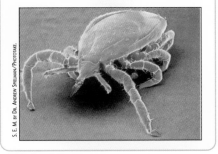

S. E. M. BY DR. ANDREW SPIELMAN/PHOTOTAKE.

PHOTO BY DR. DENNIS KUNKEL, UNIVERSITY OF HAWAII.

The head of an American dog tick, *Dermacentor variabilis*, enlarged and colorized for effect.

123

The mange mite, *Psoroptes bovis*, can infest cattle and other domestic animals.

Photo by James Hayden/Youav Phototake.

mites live in the dog's hair follicles and sebaceous glands in larger-than-normal numbers. This type of mange is commonly passed from the dam to her puppies and usually shows up on the puppies' muzzles, though demodicosis is not transferable from one normal dog to another. Most dogs recover from this type of mange without any treatment, though topical therapies are commonly prescribed by the vet.

The *Cheyletiellosis* mite is the hook-mouthed culprit associated with "walking dandruff," a condition that affects dogs as well as cats and rabbits. This mite lives on the surface of the animal's skin and is readily transferable through direct or indirect contact with an affected animal. The dandruff is present in the form of scaly skin, which may or may not be itchy. If not treated, this mange can affect a whole kennel of dogs and can be spread to humans as well.

The *Sarcoptes* mite causes intense itching on the dog in the form of a condition known as scabies or sarcoptic mange. The cycle of the *Sarcoptes* mite lasts about three weeks, and the mites live in the top layer of the dog's skin (epidermis), preferably in areas with little hair. Scabies is highly contagious and can be passed to humans. Sometimes an

Human lice look like dog lice; the two are closely related.

Photo by Dwight R. Kuhn.

allergic reaction to the mite worsens the severe itching associated with sarcoptic mange.

Ear mites, *Otodectes cynotis,* lead to otodectic mange, which most commonly affects the outer ear canal of the dog, though other areas can be affected as well. Dogs with ear-mite infestation commonly scratch at their ears, causing further irritation, and shake their heads. Dark brown droppings in the outer ear confirm the diagnosis. Your vet can prescribe a treatment to flush out the ears and kill any eggs in the ears. A complete month of treatment is necessary to cure the mange.

Two other mites, less common in dogs, include *Dermanyssus gallinae* (the poultry or red mite) and *Eutrombicula alfreddugesi* (the North American mite associated with trombiculidiasis or chigger infestation). The poultry mite frequently lives on chickens, but can transfer to dogs who spend time near farm animals. Chigger infestation affects dogs in the Central US who have

NOT A DROP TO DRINK

Never allow your dog to swim in polluted water or public areas where water quality can be suspect. Even perfectly clear water can harbor parasites, many of which can cause serious to fatal illnesses in canines. Areas inhabited by waterfowl and other wildlife are especially dangerous.

exposure to woodlands. The types of mange caused by both of these mites are treatable by vets.

INTERNAL PARASITES
Most animals—fishes, birds and mammals, including dogs and humans—have worms and other parasites that live inside their bodies. According to Dr. Herbert R. Axelrod, the fish pathologist, there are two kinds of parasites: dumb and smart. The smart parasites live in peaceful cooperation with their hosts (symbiosis), while the dumb parasites kill their hosts. Most worm infections are relatively easy to control. If they are not controlled, they weaken the host dog to the point that other medical problems occur, but they do not kill the host as dumb parasites would.

A brown dog tick, *Rhipicephalus sanguineus*, is an uncommon but annoying tick found on dogs.

PHOTO BY CAROLINA BIOLOGICAL SUPPLY/PHOTOTAKE.

DO NOT MIX

Never mix parasite-control products without first consulting your vet. Some products can become toxic when combined with others and can cause fatal consequences.

125

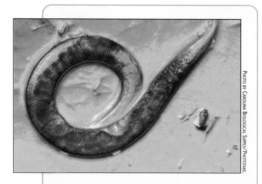

The roundworm *Rhabditis* can infect both dogs and humans.

ROUNDWORMS

Average-size dogs can pass 1,360,000 roundworm eggs every day. For example, if there were only 1 million dogs in the world, the world would be saturated with thousands of tons of dog feces. These feces would contain around 15,000,000,000 roundworm eggs.

Up to 31% of home yards and children's sand boxes in the US contain roundworm eggs.

Flushing dog's feces down the toilet is not a safe practice because the usual sewage treatments do not destroy roundworm eggs.

Infected puppies start shedding roundworm eggs at three weeks of age. They can be infected by their mother's milk.

The roundworm, *Ascaris lumbricoides.*

ROUNDWORMS

The roundworms that infect dogs are known scientifically as *Toxocara canis.* They live in the dog's intestines and shed eggs continually. It has been estimated that a dog produces about 6 or more ounces of feces every day. Each ounce of feces averages hundreds of thousands of roundworm eggs. There are no known areas in which dogs roam that do not contain roundworm eggs. The greatest danger of roundworms is that they infect people, too! It is wise to have your dog tested regularly for roundworms.

In young puppies, roundworms cause bloated bellies, diarrhea, coughing and vomiting, and are transmitted from the dam (through blood or milk). Affected puppies will not appear as animated as normal puppies. The worms appear spaghetti-like, measuring as long as 6 inches. Adult dogs can acquire roundworms through coprophagia (eating contaminated feces) or by killing rodents that carry roundworms.

Roundworm infection can kill puppies and cause severe problems in adults, as the hatched larvae travel to the lungs and trachea through the bloodstream. Cleanliness is the best preventative for roundworms. Always pick up after your dog and dispose of feces in appropriate receptacles.

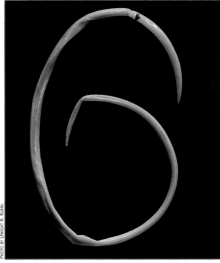

Photo by Dwight R. Kuhn

HOOKWORMS

In the United States, dog owners have to be concerned about four different species of hookworm, the most common and most serious of which is *Ancylostoma caninum,* which prefers warm climates. The others are *Ancylostoma braziliense, Ancylostoma tubaeforme* and *Uncinaria stenocephala,* the latter of which is a concern to dogs living in the Northern US and Canada, as this species prefers cold climates. Hookworms are dangerous to humans as well as to dogs and cats, and can be the cause of severe anemia due to iron deficiency. The worm uses its teeth to attach itself to the dog's intestines and changes the site of its attachment about six times per day. Each time the worm repositions itself, the dog loses blood and can become anemic. *Ancylostoma caninum* is the most likely of the four species to cause anemia in the dog.

Symptoms of hookworm infection include dark stools, weight loss, general weakness, pale coloration and anemia, as well as possible skin problems. Fortunately, hookworms are easily purged from the affected dog with a number of medications that have proven effective. Discuss these with your vet. Most heartworm preventatives include a hookworm insecticide as well.

Owners also must be aware that hookworms can infect humans, who can acquire the larvae through exposure to contaminated feces. Since the worms cannot complete their life cycle on a human, the worms simply infest the skin and cause irritation. This condition is known as cutaneous larva migrans syndrome. As a preventative, use disposable gloves or a "poop-scoop" to pick up your dog's droppings and prevent your dog (or neighborhood cats) from defecating in children's play areas.

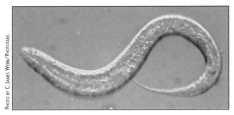

Photo by C. James Webb/Phototake.

The infective stage of the hookworm larva.

127

TAPEWORMS

Humans, rats, squirrels, foxes, coyotes, wolves and domestic dogs are all susceptible to tapeworm infection. Except in humans, tapeworms are usually not a fatal infection. Infected individuals can harbor 1000 parasitic worms.

Tapeworms, like some other types of worm, are hermaphroditic, meaning male and female in the same worm.

If dogs eat infected rats or mice, or anything else infected with tapeworm, they get the tapeworm disease. One month after attaching to a dog's intestine, the worm starts shedding eggs. These eggs are infective immediately. Infective eggs can live for a few months without a host animal.

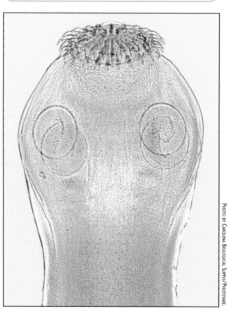

The head and rostellum (the round prominence on the scolex) of a tapeworm, which infects dogs and humans.

PHOTO BY CAROLINA BIOLOGICAL SUPPLY/PHOTOTAKE

TAPEWORMS

There are many species of tapeworm, all of which are carried by fleas! The most common tapeworm affecting dogs is known as *Dipylidium caninum*. The dog eats the flea and starts the tapeworm cycle. Humans can also be infected with tapeworms—so don't eat fleas! Fleas are so small that your dog could pass them onto your hands, your plate or your food and thus make it possible for you to ingest a flea that is carrying tapeworm eggs.

While tapeworm infection is not life-threatening in dogs (smart parasite!), it can be the cause of a very serious liver disease for humans. About 50% of the humans infected with *Echinococcus multilocularis*, a type of tapeworm that causes alveolar hydatid, perish.

WHIPWORMS

In North America, whipworms are counted among the most common parasitic worms in dogs. The whipworm's scientific name is *Trichuris vulpis*. These worms attach themselves in the lower parts of the intestine, where they feed. Affected dogs may only experience upset tummies, colic and diarrhea. These worms, however, can live for months or years in the dog, beginning their larval stage in the small intestine, spending their adult stage in the large intestine and finally passing infective eggs through the dog's feces. The only way to detect whipworms is through a fecal examination, though this is not always foolproof. Treatment for whipworms is tricky, due to the worms' unusual life-cycle pattern, and very often dogs are reinfected due to exposure to infective eggs on the ground. The whipworm eggs can survive in the environment for as long as five years; thus, cleaning up droppings in your own backyard as well as in public places is absolutely essential for sanitation purposes and the health of your dog and others.

THREADWORMS

Though less common than roundworms, hookworms and those previously mentioned,

threadworms concern dog owners in the Southwestern US and Gulf Coast area where the climate is hot and humid. Living in the small intestine of the dog, this worm measures a mere 2 millimeters and is round in shape. Like that of the whipworm, the threadworm's life cycle is very complex and the eggs and larvae are passed through the feces. A deadly disease in humans, *Strongyloides* readily infects people, and the handling of feces is the most common means of transmission. Threadworms are most often seen in young puppies; bloody diarrhea and pneumonia are symptoms. Sick puppies must be isolated and treated immediately; vets recommend a follow-up treatment one month later.

HEARTWORM PREVENTATIVES

There are many heartworm preventatives on the market, many of which are sold at your veterinarian's office. These products can be given daily or monthly, depending on the manufacturer's instructions. All of these preventatives contain chemical insecticides directed at killing heartworms, which leads to some controversy among dog owners. In effect, heartworm preventatives are necessary evils, though you should determine how necessary based on your pet's lifestyle. There is no doubt that heartworm is a dreadful disease that threatens the lives of dogs. However, the likelihood of your dog's being bitten by an infected mosquito is slim in most places, and a mosquito-repellent (or an herbal remedy such as Wormwood or Black Walnut) is much safer for your dog and will not compromise his immune system (the way heartworm preventatives will). Should you decide to use the traditional preventative "medications," you can consider giving the pill every other or third month. Since the toxins in the pill will kill the heartworms at all stages of development, the pill would be effective in killing larvae, nymphs or adults, and it takes four months for the larvae to reach the adult stage. Thus, there is no rationale to poisoning the dog's system on a monthly basis. Lastly, do not give the pill during the winter months, since there are no mosquitoes around to pass on their infection, unless you live in a tropical environment.

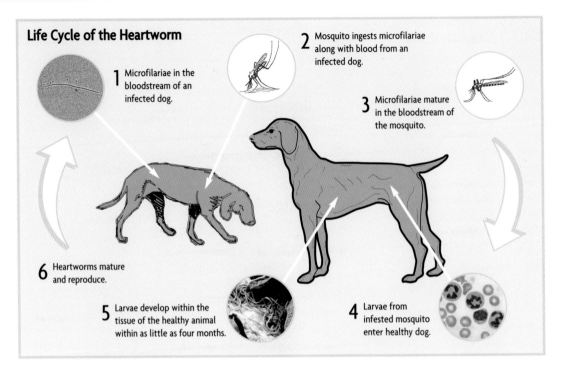

Life Cycle of the Heartworm

1 Microfilariae in the bloodstream of an infected dog.

2 Mosquito ingests microfilariae along with blood from an infected dog.

3 Microfilariae mature in the bloodstream of the mosquito.

6 Heartworms mature and reproduce.

5 Larvae develop within the tissue of the healthy animal within as little as four months.

4 Larvae from infested mosquito enter healthy dog.

HEARTWORMS

Heartworms are thin, extended worms up to 12 inches long, which live in a dog's heart and the major blood vessels surrounding it. Dogs may have up to 200 worms. Symptoms may be loss of energy, loss of appetite, coughing, the development of a pot belly and anemia.

Heartworms are transmitted by mosquitoes. The mosquito drinks the blood of an infected dog and takes in larvae with the blood. The larvae, called microfilariae, develop within the body of the mosquito and are passed on to the next dog bitten after the larvae mature. It takes two to three weeks for the larvae to develop to the infective stage within the body of the mosquito. Dogs are usually treated at about six weeks of age and maintained on a prophylactic dose given monthly.

Blood testing for heartworms is not necessarily indicative of how seriously your dog is infected. Although this is a dangerous disease, it is not easy for a dog to be infected. Discuss the various preventatives with your vet, as there are many different types now available. Together you can decide on a safe course of prevention for your dog.

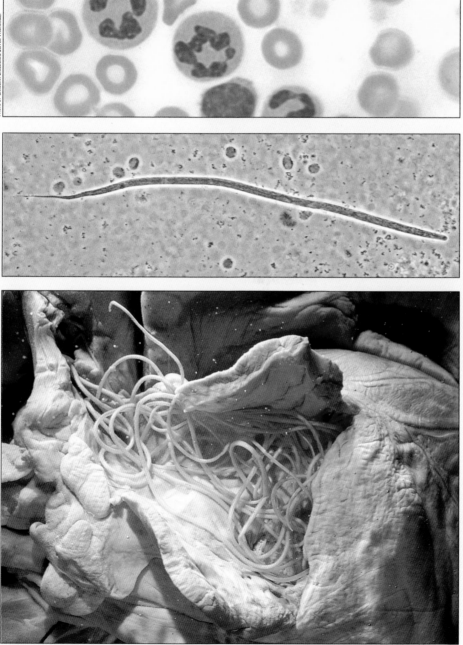

Magnified
heartworm larvae,
Dirofilaria immitis.

Heartworm,
*Dirofilaria
immitis.*

The heart
of a dog infected
with canine
heartworm,
*Dirofilaria
immitis.*

Chihuahua

HOMEOPATHY:
an alternative
to medicine

"Less is Most"

Using this principle, the strength of a homeopathic remedy is measured by the number of serial dilutions that were undertaken to create it. The greater the number of serial dilutions, the greater the strength of the homeopathic remedy. The potency of a remedy that has been made by making a dilution of 1 part in 100 parts (or 1/100) is 1c or 1cH. If this remedy is subjected to a series of further dilutions, each one being 1/100, a more dilute and stronger remedy is produced. If the remedy is diluted in this way six times, it is called 6c or 6cH. A dilution of 6c is 1 part in 1000,000,000,000. In general, higher potencies in more frequent doses are better for acute symptoms and lower potencies in more infrequent doses are more useful for chronic, long-standing problems.

CURING YOUR DOG NATURALLY

Holistic medicine means treating the whole animal as a unique, perfect living being. Generally, holistic treatments do not suppress the symptoms that the body naturally produces, as do most medications prescribed by conventional doctors and vets. Holistic methods seek to cure disease by regaining balance and harmony in the patient's environment. Some of these methods include use of nutritional therapy, herbs, flower essences, aromatherapy, acupuncture, massage, chiropractic and, of course the most popular holistic approach, homeopathy.

Homeopathy is a theory or system of treating illness with small doses of substances which, if administered in larger quantities, would produce the symptoms that the patient already has. This approach is often described as "like cures like." Although modern veterinary medicine is geared toward the "quick fix," homeopathy relies on the belief that, given the time, the body is able to heal itself and return to its natural, healthy state.

Choosing a remedy to cure a problem in our dogs is the difficult part of homeopathy. Consult with your veterinarian for a professional diagnosis of your dog's symptoms. Often these symptoms require

immediate conventional care. If your vet is willing, and knowledge-able, you may attempt a homeopathic remedy. Be aware that cortisone prevents homeopathic remedies from working. There are hundreds of possibilities and combinations to cure many problems in dogs, from basic physical problems such as excessive shedding, fleas or other parasites, unattractive doggy odor, bad breath, upset stomach, obesity, dry, oily or dull coat, diarrhea, ear problems or eye discharge (including tears and dry or mucusy matter), to behavioral abnormalities such as fear of loud noises, habitual licking, poor appetite, excessive barking and various phobias. From alumina to zincum metallicum, the remedies span the planet and the imagination…from flowers and weeds to chemicals, insect droppings, diesel smoke and volcanic ash.

Using "Like to Treat Like"

Unlike conventional medicines that suppress symptoms, homeopathic remedies treat illnesses with small doses of substances that, if administered in larger quantities, would produce the symptoms that the patient already has. While the same homeopathic remedy can be used to treat different symptoms in different dogs, here are some interesting remedies and their uses.

Apis Mellifica
(made from honey bee venom) can be used for allergies or to reduce swelling that occurs in acutely infected kidneys.

Diesel Smoke
can be used to help control motion sickness.

Calcarea Fluorica
(made from calcium fluoride, which helps harden bone structure) can be useful in treating hard lumps in tissues.

Natrum Muriaticum
(made from common salt, sodium chloride) is useful in treating thin, thirsty dogs.

Nitricum Acidum
(made from nitric acid) is used for symptoms you would expect to see from contact with acids such as lesions, especially where the skin joins the linings of body orifices or openings such as the lips and nostrils.

Symphytum
(made from the herb Knitbone, *Symphytum officianale*) is used to encourage bones to heal.

Urtica Urens
(made from the common stinging nettle) is used in treating painful, irritating rashes.

HOMEOPATHIC REMEDIES FOR YOUR DOG

Symptom/Ailment	Possible Remedy
ALLERGIES	Apis Mellifica 30c, Astacus Fluviatilis 6c, Pulsatilla 30c, Urtica Urens 6c
ALOPECIA	Alumina 30c, Lycopodium 30c, Sepia 30c, Thallium 6c
ANAL GLANDS (BLOCKED)	Hepar Sulphuris Calcareum 30c, Sanicula 6c, Silicea 6c
ARTHRITIS	Rhus Toxicodendron 6c, Bryonia Alba 6c
CANINE COUGH	Drosera 6c, Ipecacuanha 30c
CATARACT	Calcarea Carbonica 6c, Conium Maculatum 6c, Phosphorus 30c, Silicea 30c
CONSTIPATION	Alumina 6c, Carbo Vegetabilis 30c, Graphites 6c, Nitricum Acidum 30c, Silicea 6c
COUGHING	Aconitum Napellus 6c, Belladonna 30c, Hyoscyamus Niger 30c, Phosphorus 30c
DIARRHEA	Arsenicum Album 30c, Aconitum Napellus 6c, Chamomilla 30c, Mercurius Corrosivus 30c
DRY EYE	Zincum Metallicum 30c
EAR PROBLEMS	Aconitum Napellus 30c, Belladonna 30c, Hepar Sulphuris 30c, Tellurium 30c, Psorinum 200c
EYE PROBLEMS	Borax 6c, Aconitum Napellus 30c, Graphites 6c, Staphysagria 6c, Thuja Occidentalis 30c
GLAUCOMA	Aconitum Napellus 30c, Apis Mellifica 6c, Phosphorus 30c
HEAT STROKE	Belladonna 30c, Gelsemium Sempervirens 30c, Sulphur 30c
HICCOUGHS	Cinchona Deficinalis 6c
HIP DYSPLASIA	Colocynthis 6c, Rhus Toxicodendron 6c, Bryonia Alba 6c
INCONTINENCE	Argentum Nitricum 6c, Causticum 30c, Conium Maculatum 30c, Pulsatilla 30c, Sepia 30c
INSECT BITES	Apis Mellifica 30c, Cantharis 30c, Hypericum Perforatum 6c, Urtica Urens 30c
ITCHING	Alumina 30c, Arsenicum Album 30c, Carbo Vegetabilis 30c, Hypericum Perforatum 6c, Mezerium 6c, Sulphur 30c
MASTITIS	Apis Mellifica 30c, Belladonna 30c, Urtica Urens 1m
MOTION SICKNESS	Cocculus 6c, Petroleum 6c
PATELLAR LUXATION	Gelsemium Sempervirens 6c, Rhus Toxicodendron 6c
PENIS PROBLEMS	Aconitum Napellus 30c, Hepar Sulphuris Calcareum 30c, Pulsatilla 30c, Thuja Occidentalis 6c
PUPPY TEETHING	Calcarea Carbonica 6c, Chamomilla 6c, Phytolacca 6c

Recognizing a Sick Dog

Unlike colicky babies and cranky children, our canine kids cannot tell us when they are feeling ill. Therefore, there are a number of signs that owners can identify to know that their dogs are not feeling well.

Take note for physical manifestations such as:

- unusual, bad odor, including bad breath
- excessive shedding
- wax in the ears, chronic ear irritation
- oily, flaky, dull haircoat
- mucus, tearing or similar discharge in the eyes
- fleas or mites
- mucus in stool, diarrhea
- sensitivity to petting or handling
- lack of appetite, digestive problems

Keep an eye out for behavioral changes as well including:

- lethargy, idleness
- lack of patience or general irritability
- licking at paws, scratching face, etc.
- phobias (fear of people, loud noises, etc.)
- strange behavior, suspicion, fear
- coprophagia
- more frequent barking
- whimpering, crying

Get Well Soon

You don't need a DVM to provide good TLC to your sick or recovering dog, but you do need to pay attention to some details that normally wouldn't bother him. The following tips will aid Fido's recovery and get him back on his paws again:

- Keep his space free of irritating smells, like heavy perfumes and air fresheners.
- Rest is the best medicine! Avoid harsh lighting that will prevent your dog from sleeping. Shade him from bright sunlight during the day and dim the lights in the evening.
- Keep the noise level down. Animals are more sensitive to sound when they are sick.

- Be attentive to any necessary temperature adjustments. A dog with a fever needs a cool room and cold liquids. A bitch that is whelping or recovering from surgery will be more comfortable in a warm room, consuming warm liquids and food.
- You wouldn't send a sick child back to school early, so don't rush your dog back into a full routine until he seems absolutely ready.

The eyes of a Chihuahua should be clear, showing no signs of irritation or debris.

A DOG OWNER'S GUIDE TO COMMON OPHTHALMIC DISEASES
by Prof. Dr. Robert L. Peiffer, Jr.

Few would argue that vision is the most important of the cognitive senses, and maintenance of a normal visual system is important for an optimal quality of life. Likewise, pet owners tend to be acutely aware of their pet's eyes and vision, which is important because early detection of ocular disease will optimize therapeutic outcomes. The eye is a sensitive organ with minimal reparative capabilities, and with some diseases, such as glaucoma, uveitis and retinal detachment, early diagnosis and treatment can be critical in terms of whether vision can be preserved.

Lower entropion, or rolling in of the eyelid, is causing irritation in the left eye of this young dog. Several extra eyelashes, or distichiasis, are present on the upper lid.

The causes of ocular disease are quite varied; the nature of dogs make them susceptible to traumatic conditions, the most common of which include proptosis of the globe, cat-scratch injuries and penetrating wounds from foreign objects, including sticks and BB gun pellets. Infectious diseases caused by bacteria, viruses or fungi may be localized to the eye or part of a systemic infection. Many of the common conditions, including eyelid conformational problems, cataracts, glaucoma and retinal degenerations have a genetic basis.

Before acquiring your puppy, it is important to ascertain that both parents have been examined and certified free of eye disease by a veterinary ophthalmologist. Since many of these genetic diseases can be detected early in life, acquire the pup with the condition that it pass a thorough ophthalmic examination by a qualified specialist.

LID CONFORMATIONAL ABNORMALITIES
Rolling in (entropion) or out (ectropion) of the lids tends to be a breed-related problem. Entropion can involve the upper and/or lower lids. Signs usually appear between 3 and 12 months of age. The irritation caused by the eyelid hairs' rubbing

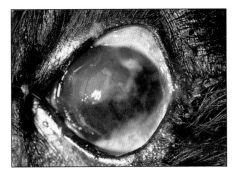

on the surface of the cornea may result in blinking, tearing and damage to the cornea. Ectropion is likewise breed-related and is considered "normal" in hounds, for instance; unlike entropion, which results in acute discomfort, ectropion may cause chronic irritation related to exposure and the pooling of secretions. Most of these cases can be managed medically with daily irrigation with sterile saline and topical antibiotics when required.

EYELASH ABNORMALITIES
Dogs normally have lashes only on the upper lids, in contrast to humans. Occasionally, extra eyelashes may be seen emerging at the eyelid margin (distichiasis) or through the inner surface of the eyelid (ectopic cilia).

CONJUNCTIVITIS
Inflammation of the conjunctiva, the pink tissue that lines the lids and the anterior portion of the sclera, is generally accompanied by redness, discharge and mild discomfort. The majority of cases are either associated with bacterial infections or dry eye syndrome. Fortunately, topical medications are generally effective in curing or controlling the problem.

DRY EYE SYNDROME
Dry eye syndrome (keratoconjunctivitis sicca) is a common cause of external ocular disease. Discharge is typically thick and sticky, and keratitis is a frequent component; any breed can be affected. While some cases can be associated with toxic effects of drugs, including the sulfa antibiotics, the cause in the majority of the cases cannot be determined and is assumed to be immune-mediated.

Keratoconjunctivitis sicca, seen here in the right eye of a middle-aged dog, causes a characteristic thick mucus discharge as well as secondary corneal changes.

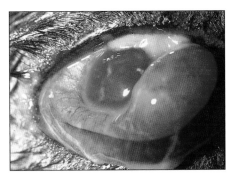

Left: Prolapse of the gland of the third eyelid in the right eye of a pup. Right: In this case, in the right eye of a young dog, the prolapsed gland can be seen emerging between the edge of the third eyelid and the corneal surface.

Chihuahua

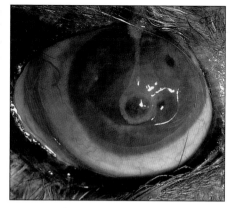

Multiple deep ulcerations affect the cornea of this middle-aged dog.

PROLAPSE OF THE GLAND OF THE THIRD EYELID

In this condition, commonly referred to as *cherry eye*, the gland of the third eyelid, which produces about one-third of the aqueous phase of the tear film and is normally situated within the anterior orbit, prolapses to emerge as a pink fleshy mass protruding over the edge of the third eyelid, between the third eyelid and the cornea. The condition usually develops during the first year of life and, while mild irritation may result, the condition is unsightly as much as anything else.

Lipid deposition can occur as a primary inherited dystrophy, or secondarily to hypercholesterolemia (in dogs frequently associated with hypothyroidism), chronic corneal inflammation or neoplasia. The deposits in this dog assume an oval pattern in the center of the cornea.

CORNEAL DISEASE

The cornea is the clear front part of the eye that provides the first step in the collection of light on its journey to be eventually focused onto the retina, and most corneal diseases will be manifested by alterations in corneal transparency. The cornea is an exquisitely innervated

138

tissue, and defects in corneal integrity are accompanied by pain, which is demonstrated by squinting.

Corneal ulcers may occur secondarily to trauma or to irritation from entropion or ectopic cilia. In middle-aged or older dogs, epithelial ulcerations may occur spontaneously due to an inherent defect; these are referred to as indolent or Boxer ulcers, in recognition of the breed in which we see the condition most frequently. Infection may occur secondarily. Ulcers can be potentially blinding conditions; severity is dependent upon the size and depth of the ulcer and other complicating features.

Non-ulcerative keratitis tends to have an immune-mediated component and is managed by topical immunosuppressants, usually corticosteroids. Corneal edema can occur in elderly dogs. It is due to a failure of the corneal endothelial "pump."

The cornea responds to chronic irritation by transforming

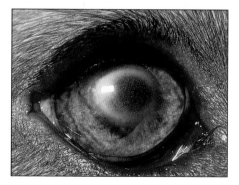

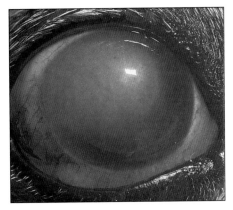

into skin-like tissue that is evident clinically by pigmentation, scarring and vascularization; some cases may respond to tear stimulants, lubricants and topical corticosteroids, while others benefit from surgical narrowing of the eyelid opening in order to enhance corneal protection.

UVEITIS
Inflammation of the vascular tissue of the eye–the uvea—is a common and potentially serious disease in dogs. While it may occur secondarily to trauma or other intraocular diseases, such as

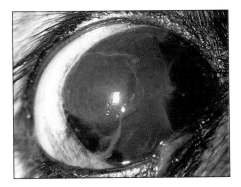

cataracts, most commonly uveitis is associated with some type of systemic infectious or neoplastic process. Uncontrolled, uveitis can lead to blinding cataracts, glaucoma and/or retinal detachments, and aggressive symptomatic therapy with dilating agents (to prevent pupillary adhesions) and anti-inflammatories are critical.

GLAUCOMA
The eye is essentially a hollow fluid-filled sphere, and the pressure within is maintained by regulation of the rate of fluid production and fluid egress at 10–20 mms of mercury. The retinal cells are extremely sensitive to elevations of intraocular pressure and, unless controlled, permanent blindness can occur within hours to days. In acute glaucoma, the conjunctiva becomes congested, the cornea cloudy, the pupil moderate and fixed; the eye is generally painful and avisual. Increased constant signs of

Corneal edema can develop as a slowly progressive process in elderly dogs of various breeds as a result of the inability of the corneal endothelial "pump" to maintain a state of dehydration.

Medial pigmentary keratitis in this dog is associated with irritation from prominent facial folds.

139

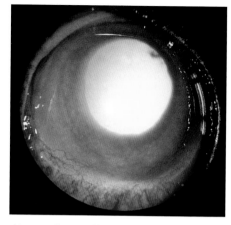

Glaucoma in the dog most commonly occurs as a sudden extreme elevation of intraocular pressure, frequently to three to four times the norm. The eye of this dog demonstrates the common signs of episcleral injection, or redness; mild diffuse corneal cloudiness, due to edema; and a mid-sized fixed pupil.

Left: The typical posterior subcapsular cataract appears between one and two years of age, but rarely progresses to where the animal has visual problems. Right: Inherited cataracts generally appear between three and six years of age, and progress to the stage seen where functional vision is significantly impaired.

discomfort will accompany chronic cases.

Management of glaucoma is one of the most challenging situations the veterinary ophthalmologist faces; in spite of intense efforts, many of these cases will result in blindness.

CATARACTS AND LENS DISLOCATION
Cataracts are the most common blinding condition in dogs; fortunately, they are readily amenable to surgical intervention, with excellent results in terms of restoration of vision and replace-

ment of the cataractous lens with a synthetic one. Most cataracts in dogs are inherited; less commonly, cataracts can be secondary to trauma or other ocular diseases, including uveitis, glaucoma, lens luxation and retinal degeneration, or secondary to an underlying systemic metabolic disease, including diabetes and Cushing's disease. Signs include a progressive loss of the bright dark appearance of the pupil, which is replaced by a blue-gray hazy appearance. In this respect, cataracts need to be distinguished from the normal aging process of nuclear sclerosis, which occurs in middle-aged or older animals and has minimal effect on vision.

Lens dislocation occurs in dogs and frequently leads to secondary glaucoma; early removal of the dislocated lens is generally effective.

RETINAL DISEASE
Retinal degenerations are usually inherited, but may be associated with vitamin E deficiency in dogs.

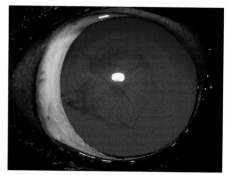

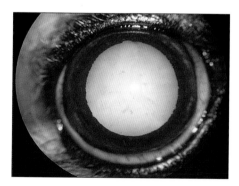

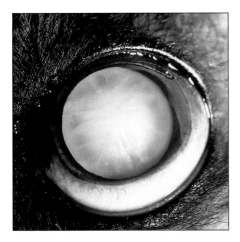

conditions, as the retinal tissues possess minimal regenerative capabilities. Most pets, however, with a bit of extra care and attention, show an amazing ability to adapt to an avisual world, and can be maintained as pets with a satisfactory quality of life.

Detachment of the retina—due to accumulation of blood between the retina and the underling uvea, which is called the *choroid*—can occur secondarily to retinal tears or holes or tractional forces within the eye, or as a result of uveitis. These types of detachments may be amenable to surgical repair if diagnosed early.

While signs are variable, most frequently one notes a decrease in vision over a period of months, which typically starts out as night blindness. The cause of a more rapid loss of vision due to retinal degeneration that occurs over days to weeks is labeled sudden acquired retinal degeneration or SARD; the outcome, however, is unfortunately usually similar to inherited and nutritional

OPTIC NEURITIS
Optic neuritis, or inflammation of the nerve that connects the eye with the brain stem, is a relatively uncommon condition that presents usually with rather sudden loss of vision and widely dilated non-responsive pupils.

Anterior lens luxation can occur as a primary disease in the terrier breeds, or secondarily to trauma. The fibers that hold the lens in place rupture and the lens may migrate through the pupil to be situated in front of the iris.

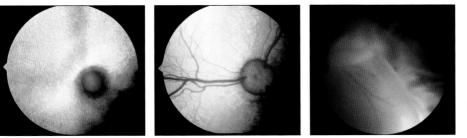

**Left: The posterior pole of a normal fundus is shown; prominent are the head of the optic nerve and the retinal blood vessels. The retina is transparent, and the prominent green tapetum is seen superiorly.
Center: An eye with inherited retinal dysplasia is depicted. The tapetal retina superior to the optic disc is disorganized, with multifocal areas of hyperplasia of the retinal pigment epithelium.
Right: Severe collie eye anomaly and a retinal detachment; this eye is unfortunately blind.**

CHIHUAHUA

The term *old* is a qualitative term. For dogs, as well as their masters, old is relative. Certainly we can all distinguish between a puppy Chihuahua and an adult Chihuahua—there are the obvious physical traits, such as size, appearance and facial expressions, as well as personality traits. Puppies and young dogs like to play with children. Children's natural exuberance is a good match for the seemingly endless energy of young dogs. They like to run, jump, chase and retrieve. When dogs grow up and cease their interaction with children, they are often thought of as being too old to play with the kids.

On the other hand, if a Chihuahua is only exposed to older people or those with quieter lifestyles, his life will normally be less active and the slowing down that comes with aging will not be as noticeable.

If people live to be 100 years old, dogs live to be 20 years old. While this is a good rule of thumb, it is very inaccurate. When trying to compare dog years to human years, you cannot make a generalization about all dogs.

You can make the generalization that 13 years is a good lifespan for a Chihuahua, which is quite good compared to many other pure-bred dogs that may only live to 8 or 9 years of age. Some Chihuahuas have been known to live to 20 years. Dogs are generally considered mature within three years, but they can reproduce even earlier. So, generally speaking, the first three years of a dog's life are like seven times that of comparable humans. That means a 3-year-old dog is like a 21-year-old human. As the curve of

CONSISTENCY COUNTS

Puppies and older dogs are very similar in their need for consistency in their lives. Older pets may experience hearing and vision loss, or may just be more easily confused by changes in their homes. Try to keep things consistent for the senior dog. For example, doors that are always open or closed should remain so. Most importantly, don't dismiss a pet just because he's getting old; most senior dogs remain active and important parts of their owners' lives.

CDS
COGNITIVE DYSFUNCTION SYNDROME
"Old-Dog Syndrome"

SYMPTOMS OF CDS

There are many ways to evaluate old-dog syndrome. Veterinarians have defined CDS (cognitive dysfunction syndrome) as the gradual deterioration of cognitive abilities. These are indicated by changes in the dog's behavior. When a dog changes his routine response, and maladies have been eliminated as the cause of these behavioral changes, then CDS is the usual diagnosis.

More than half the dogs over eight years old suffer some form of CDS. The older the dog, the more chance it has of suffering from CDS. In humans, doctors often dismiss the CDS behavioral changes as part of "winding down."

There are four major signs of CDS: frequent potty accidents inside the home, sleeps much more or much less than normal, acts confused and fails to respond to social stimuli.

FREQUENT POTTY ACCIDENTS
- *Urinates in the house.*
- *Defecates in the house.*
- *Doesn't signal that he wants to go out.*

SLEEP PATTERNS
- *Awakens more slowly.*
- *Sleeps more than normal during the day.*
- *Sleeps less during the night.*

CONFUSION
- *Goes outside and just stands there.*
- *Appears confused with a faraway look in his eyes.*
- *Hides more often.*
- *Doesn't recognize friends.*
- *Doesn't come when called.*
- *Walks around listlessly without a destination.*

FAILS TO RESPOND TO SOCIAL STIMULI
- *Comes to people less frequently, whether called or not.*
- *Doesn't tolerate petting for more than a short time.*
- *Doesn't come to the door when you return home from work.*

GETTING OLD

The bottom line is simply that your dog is getting old when you think he is getting old because he slows down in his level of general activity, including walking, running, eating, jumping and retrieving. On the other hand, the frequency of certain activities increases, such as more sleeping, more barking and more repetition of habits like going to the door without being called when you put your coat on to leave the house.

WHAT TO LOOK FOR IN SENIORS

Most veterinarians and behaviorists use the seven-year mark as the time to consider a dog a "senior." The term "senior" does not imply that the dog is geriatric and has begun to fail in mind and body. Aging is essentially a slowing process. Humans readily admit that they feel a difference in their activity level from age 20 to 30, and then from 30 to 40, etc. By treating the seven-year-old dog as a senior, owners are able to implement certain therapeutic and preventative medical strategies with the help of their veterinarians. A senior-care program should include at least two veterinary visits per year and screening sessions to determine the dog's

comparison shows, there is no hard and fast rule for comparing dog and human ages. The comparison is made even more difficult, for not all humans age at the same rate...and human females live longer than human males.

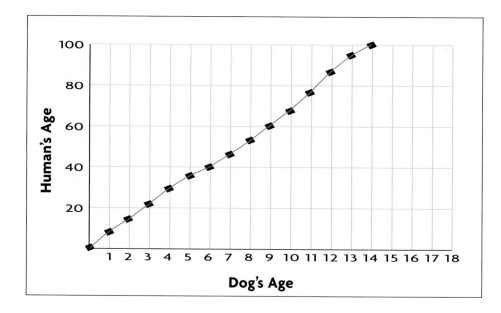

health status, as well as nutritional counseling. Veterinarians determine the senior dog's health status through a blood smear for a complete blood count, serum chemistry profile with electrolytes, urinalysis, blood pressure check, electrocardiogram, ocular tonometry (pressure on the eyeball) and dental prophylaxis.

Such an extensive program for senior dogs is well advised before owners start to see the obvious physical signs of aging, such as slower and inhibited movement, graying, increased sleep/nap periods and disinterest in play and other activity. This preventative program promises a longer, healthier life for the aging dog. Among the physical problems common in aging dogs are the loss of sight and hearing, arthritis, kidney and liver failure, diabetes mellitus, heart disease and Cushing's disease (a hormonal disease).

In addition to the physical manifestations discussed, there are some behavioral changes and problems related to aging dogs. Dogs suffering from hearing or vision loss, dental discomfort or arthritis can become aggressive. Likewise, the near-deaf and/or blind dog may be startled more easily and react in an unexpectedly aggressive manner. Seniors suffering from senility can become more impatient and

SENIOR SIGNS

An old dog starts to show one or more of the following symptoms:
- The hair on the face and paws starts to turn gray. The color breakdown usually starts around the eyes and mouth.
- Sleep patterns are deeper and longer, and the old dog is harder to awaken.
- Food intake diminishes.

- Responses to calls, whistles and other signals are ignored more and more.
- Eye contact does not evoke tail wagging (assuming it once did).

irritable. Housesoiling accidents are associated with loss of mobility, kidney problems and loss of sphincter control as well as plaque accumulation, physiological brain changes and reactions to medications. Older dogs, just like young puppies, suffer from separation anxiety, which can lead to excessive barking, whining, housesoiling and destructive behavior. Seniors may become fearful of everyday sounds, such as vacuum cleaners, heaters, thunder and passing traffic. Some dogs have difficulty sleeping, due to discomfort, the need for frequent potty visits and the like.

Owners should avoid spoiling the older dog with too many fatty treats. Obesity is a common problem in older dogs and subtracts years from their lives. Keep the senior dog as trim as possible since excess weight puts additional stress on the body's vital organs. Some breeders recommend supplementing the diet with foods high in fiber and lower in calories. Adding fresh vegetables and marrow broth to the senior's diet makes a tasty, low-calorie, low-fat supplement. Vets also offer specialty diets for senior dogs that are worth exploring.

Your ChiChi, as he nears his twilight years, needs his owner's patience and good care more than ever. Never punish an older dog

HORMONAL PROBLEMS

Although graying is normal and expected in older dogs, a flaky coat or loss of hair is not. Such coat problems may point to a hormonal problem. Hypothyroidism, in which the thyroid gland fails to produce the normal amount of hormones, is one such problem. Your veterinarian can treat hypothyroidism with an oral supplement. The condition is more common in certain breeds, so discuss its likelihood in your dog with your breeder and vet.

for an accident or abnormal behavior. For all the years of love and companionship that your dog has provided, he deserves special attention and courtesies. The older dog may need to relieve himself at 3 a.m. because he can no longer hold it for eight hours. Older dogs may not be able to remain crated for more than two or three hours. It may be time to give up a sofa or chair to your old friend. Although he may not seem as enthusiastic about your attention and petting, he does appreciate the considerations you offer as he gets older.

Your Chihuahua does not understand why his world is slowing down. Owners must make the transition into the golden years as pleasant and rewarding as possible.

WHEN THE TIME COMES

You are never fully prepared to make a rational decision about putting your dog to sleep. It is very obvious that you love your Chihuahua or you would not be reading this book. Putting a loved dog to sleep is extremely difficult. It is a decision that must be made with your veterinarian. You are usually forced to make the decision when one of the life-threatening symptoms previously mentioned becomes serious enough for you to seek veterinary help.

If the prognosis of the malady indicates the end is near and your beloved pet will only suffer more and experience no enjoyment for the balance of its life, then euthanasia is the right choice.

WHAT IS EUTHANASIA?

Euthanasia derives from the Greek, meaning *good death*. In other words, it means the planned, painless killing of a dog suffering from a painful,

EUTHANASIA

Euthanasia is a procedure that must be performed by a licensed veterinarian. There also may be societies for the prevention of cruelty to animals in your area. They often offer this service upon a vet's recommendation.

incurable condition, or who is so aged that it cannot walk, see, eat or control its excretory functions.

Euthanasia is usually accomplished by injection with an overdose of an anesthesia or barbiturate. Aside from the prick of the needle, the experience is usually painless.

MAKING THE DECISION

The decision to euthanize your dog is never easy. The days during which the dog becomes ill and the end occurs can be unusually stressful for you. If this is your first experience with the death of a loved one, you may need the comfort dictated by your religious beliefs. If you are the head of the family and have children, you should have involved them in the decision of putting your Chihuahua to sleep. Usually your dog can be maintained on drugs for a few days in order to give you ample time to make a decision. During this time, talking with members of your family or even people who have lived through this same experience can ease the burden of your inevitable decision.

THE FINAL RESTING PLACE

Dogs can have some of the same privileges as humans. The remains of your beloved dog can be buried in a pet cemetery, which is generally expensive though not beyond the reach of

Pet cemeteries are usually located near cities and suburban areas. Ask your veterinarian for his advice.

GETTING ANOTHER DOG?

The grief of losing your beloved Chihuahua will be as lasting as the grief of losing a human friend or relative. In most cases, if your dog died of old age, it had slowed down considerably. Do you want a new Chihuahua puppy to replace it? Or are you better off finding a more mature Chihuahua, say two to three years of age, which will usually be house-trained and will have an already developed personality. In this case, you can find out if you like each other after a few hours of being together.

The decision is, of course, your own. Do you want another Chihuahua or perhaps a different breed so as to avoid comparison with your beloved friend? Most people usually buy the same breed because they know (and love) the characteristics of that breed. Then, too, they often know people who have the same breed and perhaps they are lucky enough that one of their friends expects a litter soon. What could be better?

most owners. Dogs who have died at home can be buried in your yard in a place suitably marked with a stone or newly planted tree or bush. Alternatively, your dog can be cremated individually and the ashes returned to you. A less expensive option is mass cremation, although, of course, the ashes cannot then be returned. Vets can usually arrange the cremation on your behalf. The cost of these options should always be discussed frankly and openly with your vet.

There are areas in pet cemeteries where your dog's ashes can be stored.

148

SHOWING YOUR

CHIHUAHUA

When you purchase your Chihuahua, you will make it clear to the breeder whether you want one just as a loveable companion and pet, or if you hope to be buying a Chihuahua with show prospects. No reputable breeder will sell you a young puppy and tell you that it is *definitely* of show quality, for so much can go wrong during the early months of a puppy's development. If you plan to show, what you will hopefully have acquired is a puppy with "show potential."

To the novice, exhibiting a Chihuahua in the show ring may look easy, but it takes a lot of hard work and devotion to do top winning at a show such as the prestigious Westminster Kennel Club dog show, not to mention a little luck too!

The first concept that the canine novice learns when watching a dog show is that each dog first competes against members of its own breed. Once the judge has selected the best member of each breed (Best of Breed), that chosen dog will compete with other dogs in its group. Finally, the dogs chosen first in each group will compete for Best in Show.

SHOW QUALITY SHOWS

While you may purchase a puppy in the hope of having a successful career in the show ring, it is impossible to tell, at eight to ten weeks of age, whether your dog will be a contender. Some promising pups end up with minor to serious faults that prevent them from taking home an award, but this certainly

does not mean they can't be the best of companions for you and your family. To find out if your potential show dog is show-quality, enter him in a match to see how a judge evaluates him. You also may take the pup back to your breeder as he matures to see what the breeder might advise.

The second concept that you must understand is that the dogs are not actually compared against one another. The judge compares each dog against its breed standard, the written description of the ideal specimen that is approved by the American Kennel Club (AKC). While some early breed standards were indeed based on specific dogs that were famous or popular, many dedicated enthusiasts say that a perfect specimen, as described in the standard, has never walked into a show ring, has never been bred and, to the woe of dog breeders around the globe, does not exist. Breeders attempt to get as close to this ideal as possible with every litter, but theoretically the "perfect" dog is so elusive that it is impossible.

If you are interested in exploring the world of dog showing, your best bet is to join your local breed club or the national parent club, which is the Chihuahua Club of America. These clubs often host both regional and national specialties, shows only for Chihuahuas, which can include

AKC GROUPS

For showing purposes, the American Kennel Club divides its recognized breeds into seven groups: Sporting Dogs, Hounds, Working Dogs, Terriers, Toys, Non-Sporting Dogs and Herding Dogs.

conformation as well as obedience and agility trials. Even if you have no intention of competing with your Chihuahua, a specialty is like a festival for lovers of the breed who congregate to share their favorite topic: Chihuahuas! Clubs also send out newsletters, and some organize training days and seminars in order that people may learn more about their chosen breed. To locate the breed club closest to you, contact the American Kennel Club, which furnishes the rules and regulations for all of these events plus general dog registration and other basic requirements of dog ownership.

In the US, the American Kennel Club offers three kinds of conformation shows: an all-breed show (for all AKC-recognized breeds); a specialty show (for one breed only, usually sponsored by the parent club) and a Group show (for all breeds in the Group).

For a dog to become an AKC champion of record, the dog must accumulate 15 points at the shows from at least three different judges, including two "majors." A "major" is defined as a three-, four- or five-point win, and the number of points per win is determined by the number of dogs entered in the show on that day. Depending on the breed, the number of points that are awarded varies. In a breed as popular as the Chihuahua, more dogs are needed to rack up the points. At any dog show, only one dog and one bitch of each breed can win points.

Dog showing does not offer "co-ed" classes. Dogs and bitches never compete against each other in the classes. Non-champion dogs are called "class dogs" because they compete in one of the five classes. Dogs are entered in a particular class depending on their ages and previous show wins. To begin, there is the Puppy Class (for 6- to 9-month-olds and for 9- to 12-month-olds); this class is followed by the Novice Class (for dogs that have not won any first prizes except in the Puppy Class or three first prizes in the Novice Class and have not accumulated any points toward their champion title); the Bred-by-Exhibitor Class (for dogs handled by their breeders or handled by one of the breeder's immediate family); American-bred Class (for dogs bred in the US!); and the Open Class (for any dog that is not a champion).

The judge at the show begins judging the Puppy Class, first dogs and then bitches, and proceeds through the classes. The judge places his winners first through fourth in each class. In the Winners Class, the first-place winners of each class compete with one another to determine Winners Dog and Winners Bitch. The judge also places a Reserve Winners Dog and Reserve Winners Bitch, which could be awarded the points in the case of a disqual-ification. The Winners Dog and

Winners Bitch, the two that are awarded the points for the breed, then compete with any champions of record entered in the show. The judge reviews the Winners Dog, Winners Bitch and all the other champions to select his Best of Breed. The Best of Winners is selected between the Winners Dog

FIVE CLASSES AT SHOWS

At most AKC all-breed shows, there are five regular classes offered: Puppy, Novice, Bred by Exhibitor, American-bred and Open. The Puppy Class is usually divided as 6- to 9-months of age and 9- to 12-months of age. When deciding in which class to enter your dog, male or female, you must carefully check the show

schedule to make sure that you have selected the right class. Depending on your dog's age, previous wins and sex, you must make the best choice. It is possible to enter a one-year-old dog who has not won sufficient first places in any of the non-Puppy Classes, though the competi-tion is more intense the further you progress from the Puppy Class.

and Winners Bitch. Were one of these two to be selected Best of Breed, it would automatically be named Best of Winners as well. Finally the judge selects his Best of Opposite Sex to the Best of Breed winner.

At a Group show or all-breed show, the Best of Breed winners from each breed then compete against one another for Group One through Group Four. The judge compares each Best of Breed to its breed standard, and the dog that most closely lives up to the ideal for its breed is selected as Group One. Finally, all seven group winners (from the Toy Group, Sporting Group, Hound Group, etc.) compete for Best in Show.

To find out about dog shows in your area, you can subscribe to the American Kennel Club's monthly magazine, The *American Kennel Gazette* and the accompanying *Events Calendar*. You can also look in your local newspaper for advertisements for dog shows in your area or go on the Internet to the AKC's website, www.akc.org.

If your Chihuahua is six months of age or older and registered with the AKC, you can enter him in a dog show where the breed is offered classes. Provided that your Chihuahua does not have a disqualifying fault, he can compete. Only unaltered dogs can be entered in a dog show, so if you have spayed or neutered your Chihuahua, you

INFORMATION ON CLUBS

You can get information about dog shows from the national kennel clubs:

American Kennel Club
5580 Centerview Drive,
Raleigh, NC 27606-3390
www.akc.org

United Kennel Club
100 E. Kilgore Road
Kalamazoo, MI 49002
www.ukcdogs.com

Canadian Kennel Club
89 Skyway Ave., Suite 100
Etobicoke, Ontario
M9W 6R4 Canada
www.ckc.ca

The Kennel Club
1-5 Clarges St., Piccadilly,
London W1Y 8AB, UK
www.the-kennel-club.org.uk

cannot compete in conformation shows. The reason for this is simple. Dog shows are the main forum to prove which representatives in a breed are worthy of being bred. Only dogs that have achieved championships—the AKC "seal of approval" for quality in pure-bred dogs—should be bred. Altered dogs, however, can participate in other AKC events such as obedience trials and the Canine Good Citizen program.

Before you actually step into the ring, you would be well advised to sit back and observe the judge's ring procedure. If it is your

A Smooth
Chihuahua and a
very proud
owner, winning a
ribbon at a major
dog show.

MEET THE AMERICAN KENNEL CLUB

The AKC is the main governing body of the dog sport in the United States. Founded in 1884, the AKC consists of 500 or more independent dog clubs plus 4,500 affiliate clubs, all of which follow the AKC rules and regulations.

Additionally, the AKC maintains a registry for pure-bred dogs in the US and works to preserve the integrity of the sport and its continuation in the country. Over 1,000,000 dogs are registered each year, representing about 150 recognized breeds.

first time in the ring, do not be over-anxious and run to the front of the line. It is much better to stand back and study how the exhibitor in front of you is performing. The judge asks each handler to "stack" the dog, hopefully showing the dog off to his best advantage. The judge will observe the dog from a distance and from different angles,

and approach the dog to check his teeth, overall structure, alertness and muscle tone, as well as consider how well the dog "conforms" to the standard. Most importantly, the judge will have the exhibitor move the dog around the ring in some pattern that he should specify (another advantage to not going first, but always listen since some judges change their directions—and the judge is always right!). Finally, the judge will give the dog one last look before moving on to the next exhibitor.

If you are not in the top four in your class at your first show, do not be discouraged. Be patient and consistent, and you may eventually find yourself in a winning line-up. Remember that the winners were once in your shoes and have devoted many hours and much money to earn the placement. If you find that your dog is losing every time and never getting a nod, it may be time to consider a different dog sport or to just enjoy your Chihuahua as a pet. Parent clubs offer other events, such as agility, obedience, and more, which may be of interest to the owner of a well-trained Chihuahua.

OBEDIENCE TRIALS
Obedience trials in the US trace back to the early 1930s when organized obedience training was developed to demonstrate how well dog and owner could work

together. The pioneer of obedience trials is Mrs. Helen Whitehouse Walker, a Standard Poodle fancier, who designed a series of exercises after the Associated Sheep, Police Army Dog Society of Great Britain. Since the days of Mrs. Walker, obedience trials have grown by leaps and bounds, and today there are over 2,000 trials held in the US every year, with more than 100,000 dogs competing. Any registered AKC dog can enter an obedience trial, regardless of conformational disqualifications or neutering.

AGILITY TRIALS

Having had its origins in the UK back in 1977, AKC agility had its official beginning in the US in August 1994, when the first AKC-licensed agility trials were held. The AKC allows all registered breeds (including Miscellaneous Class breeds) to participate, providing the dog is 12 months of age or older. Agility is designed so that the handler demonstrates how well the dog can work at his side. The handler directs his dog over an obstacle course that includes jumps as well as tires, the dog walk, weave poles, pipe tunnels, collapsed tunnels, etc. While working his way through the course, the dog must keep one eye and ear on the handler and the rest of his body on the course. The handler gives verbal and hand signals to guide the dog through the course.

Agility is great fun for dog and owner, with many rewards for everyone involved. Interested owners should join a training club that has obstacles and experienced agility handlers who can introduce you and your dog to the "ropes" (and tires, tunnels, etc.).

TEMPERAMENT PLUS

Although it seems that physical conformation is the only factor considered in the show ring, temperament is also of utmost

importance. An aggressive or fearful dog should not be shown, as bad behavior will not be tolerated and may pose a threat to the judge, other exhibitors, you and your dog.

INDEX

*Page numbers in **boldface** indicate illustrations.*

My Chihuahua

PUT YOUR PUPPY'S FIRST PICTURE HERE

Dog's Name _____

Date _____ Photographer _____